Cooking Light

OOPS!

ISBN-13: 978-0-8487-3469-5
ISBN-10: 0-8487-3469-6
Library of Congress Control Number: 2012946269
Printed in the United States of America
First printing 2012

Be sure to check with your health-care provider before making any
changes in your diet.

Oxmoor House

Editorial Director: Leah McLaughlin
Creative Director: Felicity Keane
Brand Manager: Michelle Turner Aycock
Senior Editor: Heather Averett
Managing Editor: Rebecca Benton

Cooking Light® Oops!

Editor: Rachel Quinlivan West, RD
Art Director: Claire Cormany
Project Editor: Sarah H. Doss
Junior Designer: Maribeth Jones
Director, Test Kitchen: Elizabeth Tyler Austin
Assistant Directors, Test Kitchen: Julie Christopher, Julie Gunter
Recipe Developers and Testers: Wendy Ball, RD; Victoria E. Cox;
 Stefanie Maloney; Callie Nash; Leah Van Deren
Food Stylists: Margaret Monroe Dickey, Catherine Crowell Steele
Photography Director: Jim Bathie
Senior Photo Stylist: Kay E. Clarke
Photo Stylist: Mindi Shapiro Levine
Assistant Photo Stylist: Mary Louise Menendez
Production Manager: Tamara Nall Wilder
Assistant Production Manager: Diane Rose

Contributors

Contributing Writers: Erin Bishop, Laura Hoxworth
Copy Editors: Dolores Hydock, Kate Johnson
Proofreaders: Erica Midkiff, Jacqueline Giovanelli
Indexer: Mary Ann Laurens
Interns: Elana Beth Altman; Morgan Bolling; Jessica Cox, RD;
 Susan Kemp; Alicia Lavender; Sara Lyon; Staley McIlwain;
 Emily Robinson; Katie Strasser
Photographers: John Autry, Sarah Bélanger, Beau Gustafson,
 Beth Dreiling Hontzas, Mary Britton Senseney,
 Becky Luigart-Stayner
Photo Stylists: Katherine Eckert Coyne, Missie Neville Crawford,
 Anna Pollock, Leslie Simpson, Caitlin Van Horn
Food Stylist: Ana Price Kelly

Time Home Entertainment Inc.

Publisher: Jim Childs
Vice President, Strategy & Business Development:
 Steven Sandonato
Executive Director, Marketing Services: Carol Pittard
Executive Director, Retail & Special Sales: Tom Mifsud
Director, Bookazine Development & Marketing: Laura Adam
Executive Publishing Director: Joy Butts
Associate Publishing Director: Megan Pearlman
Finance Director: Glenn Buonocore
Associate General Counsel: Helen Wan

Cooking Light®

Editor: Scott Mowbray
Creative Director: Carla Frank
Executive Managing Editor: Phillip Rhodes
Executive Editor, Food: Ann Taylor Pittman
Special Publications Editor: Mary Simpson Creel, MS, RD
Senior Food Editors: Timothy Q. Cebula, Julianna Grimes
Senior Editor: Cindy Hatcher
Assistant Editor, Nutrition: Sidney Fry, MS, RD
Assistant Editors: Kimberly Holland, Phoebe Wu
Test Kitchen Director: Vanessa T. Pruett
Assistant Test Kitchen Director: Tiffany Vickers Davis
Recipe Testers and Developers: Robin Bashinsky,
 Adam Hickman, Deb Wise
Art Directors: Fernande Bondarenko, Shawna Kalish
Senior Deputy Art Director: Rachel Cardina Lasserre
Designers: Hagen Stegall, Dréa Zacharenko
Assistant Designer: Nicole Gerrity
Photo Director: Kristen Schaefer
Assistant Photo Editor: Amy Delaune
Senior Photographer: Randy Mayor
Senior Prop Stylist: Cindy Barr
Chief Food Stylist: Kellie Gerber Kelley
Food Styling Assistant: Blakeslee Wright
Production Director: Liz Rhoades
Production Editor: Hazel R. Eddins
Assistant Production Editor: Josh Rutledge
Copy Chief: Maria Parker Hopkins
Assistant Copy Chief: Susan Roberts
Research Editor: Michelle Gibson Daniels
Administrative Coordinator: Carol D. Johnson
CookingLight.com Editor: Allison Long Lowery
Nutrition Editor: Holley Johnson Grainger, MS, RD
Associate Editor/Producer: Mallory Daugherty Brasseale

To order additional publications, call
1-800-765-6400 or 1-800-491-0551.

For more books to enrich your life, visit
oxmoorhouse.com

To search, savor, and share thousands
of recipes, visit **myrecipes.com**

Cooking Light

OOPS!

Oxmoor House

CONTENTS

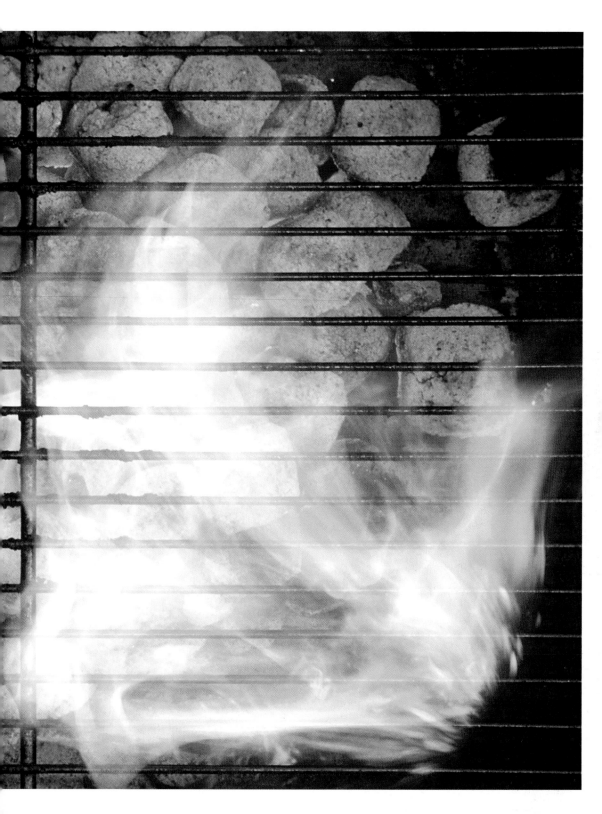

WELCOME

We all make mistakes in the kitchen, and we loved Julia Child in part because she 'fessed up and made boo-boos seem unimportant—which, in the end, they are. But it's really nice when someone else makes the mistakes. That's the idea behind this book: We blundered, you benefit.

Our good-natured Oops! stories in *Cooking Light* have always generated terrific response, because there are so many little pitfalls, disasters, and snafus possible in the complicated world of food, nutrition, cooking, and shopping. **Here we've compiled 209 cooking and nutrition errors (including a few big ones) and offered simple, visual advice on how to avoid them.** These reflect lessons we've learned the hard way over 25 years of test kitchen experimentation. Our approach has always been: Oops, laughter, lesson learned, move on. We hope you enjoy the bumpy ride, and have fun in the kitchen.

Scott Mowbray
Editor

OOPS!

GETTING STARTED

YOU DON'T READ THE ENTIRE RECIPE
before you start cooking.

THE RESULT

Flavors and textures that aren't quite right

Prepped and ready

THE FIX

Review a recipe as you would any multistep plan (because that's what it is). Even the best-written recipes don't have all the information you need in the description. Approach each recipe with a critical eye—studying, not skimming, looking for unfamiliar ingredients, specialty equipment, and potentially problematic steps. Read the recipe well before it's time to cook so you'll know if you need to marinate meats or give yeast breads sufficient time to rise. Follow the pro's habit of gathering your *mise en place*—that is, have all the ingredients gathered, prepped, and ready to go—before you turn on the heat. If you don't, you may leave out an ingredient or compromise the recipe by short changing a crucial step.

YOU USE
inferior ingredients.

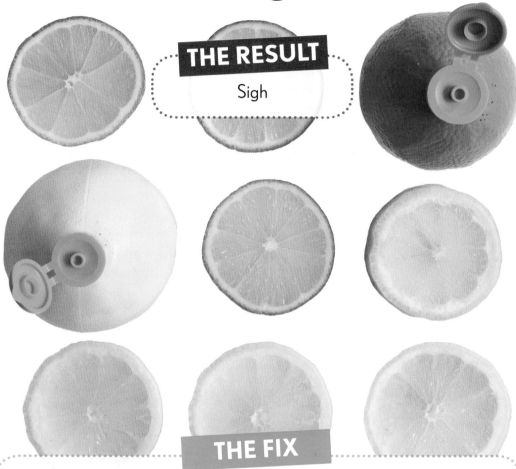

THE RESULT

Sigh

THE FIX

Good food begins and ends with the ingredients. The dishes you cook will be as mediocre, good, or superb as the ingredients they're made with. **Lower-quality substitutes simply don't taste as good, and since healthy cooking lacks the fat and sodium that can hide a plethora of mistakes, you're more likely to notice subpar ingredients.** Always buy the best ingredients—high-quality olive oil, heritage meats, imported prosciutto, fresh herbs and citrus, and real Parmigiano-Reggiano cheese—when available and affordable. They're the foundation of good cooking.

YOU ASSUME A PRODUCT WITH A HEALTH CLAIM
is healthy.

MADE WITH
ORGANIC
INGREDIENTS

Vitamin Fortified

TRANS FAT FREE

Farm Fresh!

ONLY THE BEST INGREDIENTS

CRISPY
Bits
ALL NATURAL

IMMUNITY BOOSTING

ADDED FIBER

THE RESULT

You may not be getting exactly what you think.

DELICIOUS INGREDIENTS INSIDE!

· MADE WITH ·
REAL FRUIT

SUPERFOOD!

JUST A HINT OF SUGAR

IT'S ALL GOOD

GET WHAT YOU NEED

Packages are rife with all sorts of statements claiming that the product is new, improved, and better for you. Sometimes that's true, but **those claims don't always tell the full story.** Specific health claims, such as "lowers cholesterol," are usually carefully regulated, but health *implications* made on food labels get into the undefined gray area of packaging. Here's a primer:

CLAIM: "Natural"

With no formal FDA regulation, this term can mean pretty much anything. Genetically modified foods can claim natural rights, as can "minimally processed" chicken injected with salty broth. It's up to you to define "natural." Scan the ingredients. Keep in mind that names for some additives—such as ascorbic acid (aka vitamin C) or carrageenan (a thickener made from seaweed)—sound more off-putting than they actually are.

CLAIM: "Added Fiber"

These days, fiber is popping up in unexpected foods like yogurt and ice cream. Usually this added fiber comes from inulin, polydextrose, and maltodextrin. There's nothing wrong with these, but bear in mind that they don't yet have the same history of proven benefits as fiber found naturally in foods like whole grains, beans, and fruits.

CLAIM: "Made with Real Fruit"

Some seemingly fruity foods may contain as little as 2% real fruit. Or the fruit may be juice concentrate, a form of sugar. Check the ingredients to see how far down the real fruit falls on the list.

CLAIM: "Made with Organic Ingredients"

Regulations are in place for this one. "Made with" means that products must contain at least 70% organic ingredients. The other 30% is up for grabs, though. The official USDA Organic seal appears only on foods that are 100% organic.

CLAIM: "Trans Fat Free"

According to FDA guidelines, foods making this claim can still contain up to half a gram of trans fat per serving. If partially hydrogenated oils are in the ingredient list, the product contains trans fats. (Fully hydrogenated oils are ok.) With a 2g-per-day limit, even a hidden half-gram counts. Read the label, and make the call.

YOU USE
dull knives.

THE RESULT

It's an accident waiting to happen.

You're looking sharp.

THE FIX

Though it may seem counterintuitive, sharper knives can mean fewer accidents in the kitchen. It's simply because **a dull knife requires more effort to use—it makes it harder to slice a tomato or trim a tenderloin, which can lead to slip-ups and cuts.** Use a sharpening steel (often included in knife sets) to keep knives sharp at home, or have them professionally sharpened every 6 months.

Proper storage helps keep edges sharp. The separate slots in a knife block or tray keep knives from bumping into each other. If you store them loose in a drawer, use knife covers. Wall-mounted magnetic strips are another option.

Thanks

YOU WASH YOUR KNIVES
in the dishwasher.

Dishwasher destruction

THE RESULT

Dullsville

THE FIX

A dishwasher's high-pressure jets can cause knives to bump against other utensils, damaging and dulling them over time, even when they're stored in a specially designed knife rack. The high-heat drying cycle can also warp handles. Instead, **wash knives by hand in hot water with a mild liquid dishwashing detergent, and dry them immediately to avoid stains and spots.**

YOU USE DRY AND LIQUID MEASURING CUPS interchangeably.

THE RESULT

Inaccurate measurements

THE FIX

One reason to use the proper cup is kitchen tidiness. Liquid measuring cups are usually glass or plastic with a handle and a spout. They allow you to pour the liquid so that it reaches the measurement line without overflowing. Dry measuring cups hold the exact amount and are designed to be leveled off with a flat edge—filling the cup with liquid can easily result in spillage.

Here's the bigger issue: ounces. **Liquid measuring cups indicate that 1 cup equals 8 ounces, but really it means 1 cup of *liquid* equals 8 fluid ounces. *Dry* ingredients like flour and sugar vary in weight.** For example, 1 cup of all-purpose flour weighs 4.5 ounces, not 8. For dry ingredients, weigh the ingredient or use the dry cup measurement called for in the ingredient list to make sure you get the correct amount.

STICKY INGREDIENTS
leave your utensils a mess.

THE RESULT

An annoying cleanup

THE FIX

When measuring sticky ingredients, such as honey, molasses, or syrup, **avoid the mess by coating the measuring cup or spoon with cooking spray before you measure.** The sticky ingredient will slide right out, ensuring you get the right amount, and cleanup will be a lot easier.

YOU DON'T KNOW
your oven's quirks and idiosyncrasies.

THE RESULT

Food cooks too quickly, too slowly, or unevenly.

Here's a hot spot.

THE FIX

Ideally, every oven set to 350° would heat to 350°. But many ovens don't, including expensive ones, and some change as they age. **Always use an oven thermometer and be aware of hot spots.** If your cake layers have wavy rather than flat tops, hot spots are the problem. One way to check is the bread test. Preheat the oven to 350°. Arrange bread slices on a large jelly-roll pan or baking sheet, and place pan on the middle rack. Bake at 350° for a few minutes, and see which slices get singed—their locations mark your oven's hot spots. If you find you have a hot spot in, say, the back right corner, avoid putting pans in that location, or rotate accordingly.

YOU DON'T
preheat your oven.

THE RESULT

Uneven outcomes

THE FIX

An oven that hasn't been preheated may not drastically affect casseroles, but it will have a noticeable effect on baked goods. Placing baked goods in ovens that haven't reached the specified temperature can cause problems with texture, color, and rise. Baked goods can also end up "done" long before the rise is complete or before they've sufficiently browned. **The best advice: Always preheat to avoid having any surprises emerge from your oven.**

YOU OPEN THE OVEN
too much.

It's going to take a lot of frosting to hide this crater.

THE RESULT

Your baked goods fall flat.

THE FIX

Opening the oven door causes cold air to rush into the oven, dropping the temperature and interfering with the rise of your baked goods. **It's best not to open the door until the baked goods have fully risen and you're ready to check doneness** (ideally a few minutes before the recipe's specified time). Opening the door can also slow the cook time for other types of dishes since the oven has to heat back up after a drop in temperature. If you must take a peek, use your oven light instead.

YOU PUT big SKILLETS ON small BURNERS.

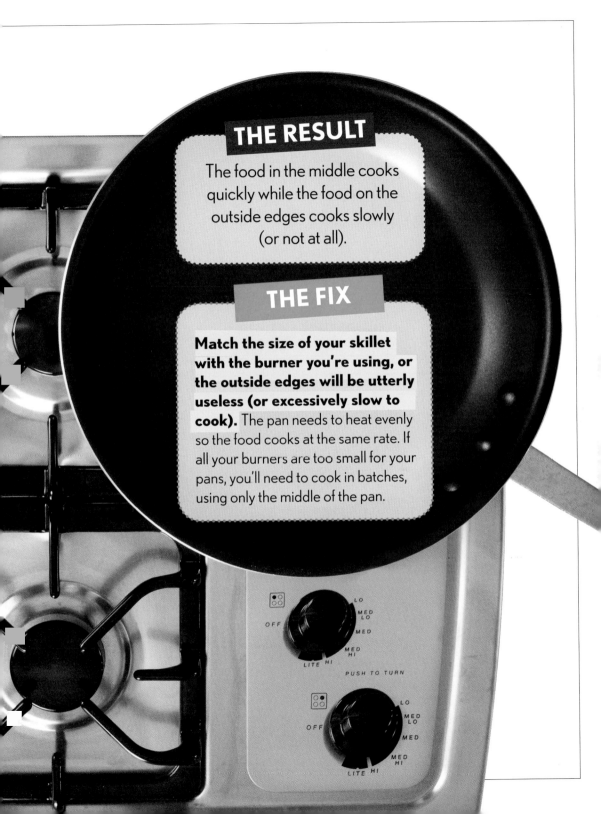

THE RESULT

The food in the middle cooks quickly while the food on the outside edges cooks slowly (or not at all).

THE FIX

Match the size of your skillet with the burner you're using, or the outside edges will be utterly useless (or excessively slow to cook). The pan needs to heat evenly so the food cooks at the same rate. If all your burners are too small for your pans, you'll need to cook in batches, using only the middle of the pan.

YOU DON'T GET THE PAN HOT ENOUGH
before you add the food.

THE RESULT

Food that sticks, scallops with no sear, pale meats

THE FIX

The inexperienced or hurried cook will barely heat the pan before adding oil and tossing in ingredients for the sauté. Next comes...nothing. Silence. No sizzle. **A hot pan is essential for sautéing vegetables or creating a great crust on meat, seafood, and poultry. It also helps keep food from sticking.** And add the oil only when the pan is hot, just before adding the ingredients. Otherwise, it will smoke, and that's bad for the oil and the food.

YOU TRASH
your rusted
cast-iron skillet.

This can be salvaged.

THE RESULT

You waste money buying a new one because the old one is perfectly fine.

Good as new

Reseasoning can revive your cast iron.

THE FIX

Evaluate how you handle your pan. **Cast iron doesn't rust because it's old or inferior; it rusts because of the way it was cared for or stored.** Some potential rust-causing situations include letting your pan sit in the sink overnight with water in it, storing it under the sink or in another moist environment, letting it air-dry, and washing it in the dishwasher. To remove the rust, use steel wool or a very fine-grade sandpaper to scour it off, and then reseason the pan. Rub the pan generously with vegetable oil. Place it in a 350° oven for 2 hours. Let it cool, and pour out residual oil. Repeat two or three times to get it completely seasoned.

YOU USE YOUR NONSTICK SKILLET for EVERYTHING.

THE RESULT

You may not be getting the best results possible.

THE FIX

Nonstick skillets are indeed versatile, but they do have limitations. They shouldn't be used at high temperatures (see page 31), and they can't go seamlessly from stovetop to oven. Other pans, like cast-iron skillets and stainless steel pans, can get very hot without damaging the pan, creating a beautiful sear on seafood and meats—results you simply can't get with a nonstick skillet.

YOU USE COOKING SPRAY AND METAL UTENSILS
with your nonstick skillet.

THE RESULT

A dinged-up pan that wears out quickly

THE FIX

Nonstick skillets are an invaluable kitchen tool, but they're not like a cast-iron skillet that can weather generations of use; these pans are fragile. When the coating becomes scratched or starts to peel, you need a new one. **Metal spoons and spatulas (and banging the pan around in the cupboard) hasten the decay of the pan.** As for cooking sprays, they're a no-no. They contain lecithin, which leaves a gummy residue that interferes with the nonstick quality.

Skip the dishwasher, too, even if the manufacturer says it's OK. Let your pan cool after use, then wash with warm, soapy water and a sponge. Avoid abrasive cleaners.

YOU COOK OVER HIGH HEAT IN
your nonstick skillet.

Toss it.

THE RESULT

High temperatures shorten the life span of your pan.

THE FIX

Use heat ranging from low to medium-high. High heat can cause the nonstick coating to discolor or lose its nonstick quality, and if the pan is heated to an extremely high temperature, the coating can give off fumes.

YOU OVERCROWD
the pan.

THE RESULT

Soggy food that doesn't brown

Steamy

THE FIX

All food releases moisture as it cooks, so you need to leave room for the steam to escape. Trapped moisture turns a browning exercise into a steam bath. If you're in a hurry, it's easy to overcrowd a pan, particularly if you're browning a large amount of meat. But those browned edges and crusty bits are critical for flavor, particularly with lower-fat cooking. Example: Putting a soggy batch of beef into a Dutch oven will not produce a beautiful, deeply flavored stew when it comes out, even if the meat gets properly tender. The same applies to crab cakes, chicken breasts, seafood, and so on. If you need to speed things up, use two pans.

YOU TURN FOOD
too often.

Put down the spatula and step away from the pan.

THE RESULT

You interfere with the sear, food sticks, or you lose the breading.

Don't try to pry food up. It'll release from the pan when it's done.

THE FIX

Leave the food alone. It's so tempting to turn, poke, and flip, but **breaded chicken or steak won't develop a nice crust unless you allow it to cook, undisturbed, for the specified time.** One sign that it's too early to turn: You can't slide a spatula cleanly under the crust.

YOUR BROILING SKILLS
are subpar.

THE RESULT

Your food is scorched
and undercooked.

| **1 min.** | **1 min. 30 sec.** | **2 min.** | **2 min. 30 sec.** |

THE FIX

When properly used, your broiler can quickly brown casseroles and gratins; sear and cook steaks, chops, and fish fillets in a flash; and toast garlic bread. It delivers a crusty exterior while preserving softness within. **Proximity to the heat is key.** You want the food near enough to the heating element for good browning action but not so close that the surface burns before the interior is done. Five inches from the broiler is a good distance, which is the second rack position from the top in most ovens—you will want to measure, though.

Timing is also key. When you set food under the broiler's intense heat, the time spent under the heat is critical—a point illustrated above with garlic bread toasted 5 inches from the heating element.

Just right

YOU ADD COLD LIQUID
to a hot glass dish.

THE RESULT

Potential breakage

THE FIX

Breakage can occur when glass undergoes sudden temperature changes. This could happen when adding a cool liquid (one that's recently been thawed or is still partially frozen) to a hot dish, or when washing a hot dish under cold water. Don't wash, refrigerate, or freeze glassware until it's completely cooled.

YOU OVERHEAT
your glass baking dishes.

THE RESULT

Your dish could break midbake.

THE FIX

Don't use glass baking dishes under the broiler or in temperatures 500° or over. At these temps, the glassware can break, ruining your meal and leaving you with a mess to clean up. Also, don't use dishes that have cracks (even tiny ones) or dings, and don't leave them on a hot burner or allow them to boil dry.

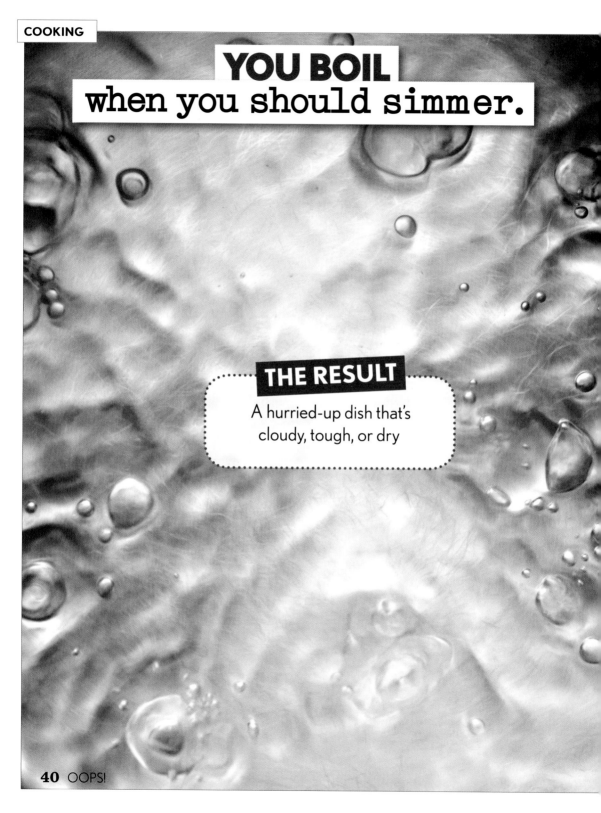

YOU BOIL
when you should simmer.

THE RESULT

A hurried-up dish that's
cloudy, tough, or dry

This is
a simmer.

THE FIX

This is one of the most common—and perhaps least recognized—kitchen errors. First, let's clarify what we mean by simmering: A bubble breaks the surface of the liquid every second or two. More vigorous bubbling means you've got a boil going. And **the difference between the two can ruin a dish.** One example: Boil a chuck roast, and it becomes tough; simmer, and the connective tissue gently melts to produce fork-tender meat.

YOU USE AN UNSAFE CONTAINER TO BOIL LIQUID in the microwave.

THE RESULT

The liquid that doesn't appear to be boiling explodes.

THE FIX

Though rare, this oops can be alarming when it does happen. When liquid is microwaved in a smooth-surfaced container, it can heat above the boiling point without actually boiling—a phenomenon known as superheating. When the liquid is jostled, it will begin bubbling violently and explode.

There's a scientific explanation for this, of course. Liquid relies on small imperfections in the vessel's surface to release bubbles (aka boiling). Without them, the liquid never boils but continues to heat, causing the temperature to rise above the boiling point. When the liquid is disturbed by a spoon or a teabag that's dropped in, all that trapped energy rises to the surface and explodes.

To prevent this, simply use an old, beat-up mug for your tea, or create a break in the surface tension by placing a popsicle stick or wooden stirrer in the container when you microwave the liquid.

YOU MICROWAVE FOOD
in plastic containers.

THE RESULT

Melted plastic

THE FIX

Plastic bags and some plastic containers aren't designed for use in the microwave. If you nuke them for too long, you'll end up with a melted mess and ruined food. **Before you hit the start button, make sure your container is microwave safe.**

As far as the safety, the jury is still out. The concern surrounds two types of chemicals commonly found in plastics—bisphenol A (BPA) and phthalates (pronounced THALates). BPA is used in many hard, clear plastics and in the lining of metal-based food and beverage cans (and has been since the 1960s), and phthalates are used in hundreds of other products, including toys, food packaging, shower curtains, and cosmetics. The worry is that a buildup of these chemicals could have adverse health effects, particularly in infants and children, but the science is not yet definitive regarding either of these chemicals. Your best bet: Use microwave-safe glass or ceramic containers to store and reheat your food to minimize exposure.

YOU ALWAYS SERVE DINNER
on your LARGEST plates.

THE RESULT

Your portions are bigger than you may think.

TOTAL
CALORIES:
830

Studies show that people eat up to 30% more when given larger portions.

THE FIX

Downsize your plates. On a standard 8- to 10-inch dinner plate, healthy portions look like a meal. On a 12- to 14-inch plate, they look meager, so if you have a fill-the-plate, clean-the-plate approach, you're likely to dish out (and consume) a bigger portion. A smaller plate automatically guides you to smaller portions.

TOTAL CALORIES: 443

TOTAL CALORIES: 443

A bigger plate makes this serving look a little stingy.

YOU EYEBALL
oil, salt, sugar.

THE RESULT

More calories or sodium than you might expect

Cooking oils—olive, canola, corn, and vegetable—all have the same amount of calories.

THE FIX

Measure. Some cookbooks call for swirls, coatings, even "glugs" of olive oil. Others, more precise, call for a teaspoon or a tablespoon—and you may be tempted just to guess. **Our experiments with guesswork, though, show that most people overpour common foods and liquids.** The difference between a teaspoon and tablespoon of any oil is 80 calories and 9g of fat. The difference between a ½ teaspoon and a teaspoon of salt is about 1,200 milligrams—half the daily recommendation.

YOU DON'T TASTE
as you go.

THE RESULT

Flavors or textures are out of balance or unappealing.

THE FIX

Recipes don't always call for the "right" amount of seasoning; cooking times are estimates; and results vary depending on your ingredients, stove, altitude, and a host of other variables. **Your palate is the control factor.** Knowing that the peaches you bought aren't that sweet tells you to boost the sugar a bit. Tasting, not time in the pot, tells you when dried beans have become tender.

No, you're not.

I'm sweet enough.

YOU STORE LEFTOVER INGREDIENTS
in the cans they came in.

THE RESULT

Off colors and flavors

THE FIX

Cans are not designed for refrigerator storage. **Refrigerating food in them can cause discoloration, particularly with acidic foods like tomato products or canned citrus.** Tinny, off flavors can also occur when oxygen causes the food to react with the metal in the can. For best results, store foods in airtight containers designed for refrigerator storage.

YOUR FOOD EMERGES FROM THE FREEZER
with freezer burn.

THE RESULT

The texture and taste of the food are off.

> Flimsy plastic or a thin bag won't protect us.

THE FIX

Those vexing ice crystals in your frozen food happen when food is stored in the freezer too long or improperly. One of the primary foes of frozen food is air, which, when trapped in the package, can cause food to dry out and can alter the taste and texture. It's not harmful, but once it's done, it's done. There's no way to reverse it.

The best way to avoid the burn: Wrap it right. Choose products designed specifically for the freezer: coated freezer paper, thick plastic freezer bags, double-seal zip-top freezer bags, and rigid plastic containers with airtight lids. Be sure to squeeze out as much air as possible, and then tightly seal. If you're going to store meats for more than a month, you'll need to double wrap the original plastic-wrapped trays.

Your potatoes have gone dry.

YOU DON'T MAKE
a game plan.

THE RESULT

Your sides are finished way before your main dish.

Hot and juicy— it might make up for the sides.

THE FIX

When preparing a meal, timing is everything. If you're hosting a dinner party, it's a good idea to create a game plan so you know when to do what to ensure everything is at the right temperature at the right time. If you don't, your side dishes may get cold sitting on the table while you're waiting for your meat to cook. **Before you start, read all your recipes through completely**—at least a day ahead of time if you're cooking for a party; then create a to-do list (as detailed as necessary). Make sure you have all the ingredients, and note the time required for each step— baking, marinating, resting—as well as the oven temperatures.

YOU DON'T KNOW WHEN
to toss the food and start over.

Got cold waiting

THE RESULT

You serve a disappointing meal. And you know it's disappointing!

THE FIX

There's no shame in making a mistake; we all do. And **while it may feel a bit wasteful to throw food in the trash, tossing out burned garlic, charred nuts, or smoking oil is the right thing to do.** Start again fresh if you have extra ingredients. Of course, there is a no-turning-back point, too. If you overcook the chicken because you didn't use a meat thermometer, you're bound to serve an overcooked chicken. At that point, the best practice is to 'fess up, apologize, pass the wine, and move on.

OOPS!

FRUITS, VEGETABLES & GRAINS

YOU BUY
fruits and vegetables out of season.

THE RESULT

You end up with bland produce.

THE FIX

In season but imperfect? Give it a chance!

Don't let picture-perfect out-of-season produce deceive you —the beauty of these fruits and vegetables really is just skin deep. Even the most amazing looking eggplant purchased in the winter is likely to be bitter and spongy, so hold off until the summer when you can really enjoy all this vegetable has to offer. This goes for all out-of-season produce. In-season fruits and vegetables really taste best.

YOU EAT VEGETABLES IN A RAINBOW OF COLORS— excluding white.

THE RESULT

You miss out on sources of antioxidants, vitamins, and minerals that could add more flavor and variety to your diet.

THE FIX

Think of white as a color, too, and enjoy white vegetables. **Cauliflower, white onion, and garlic all contain compounds linked to cancer prevention.** And even white-fleshed potatoes (with the skin on) are a healthy option: They have potassium, vitamin C, and fiber.

Out of season but beautiful? Think twice.

YOU STOCK UP ON FRESH VEGETABLES ON SUNDAY
for your week of healthy eating.

THE RESULT

Come Thursday or Friday, nutrients have done a vanishing act.

In a week, green beans lose 77% of their vitamin C, and spinach loses 50% of its folate.

THE FIX

Some nutrients begin deteriorating in a fresh fruit or vegetable as soon as it's harvested. **It may be less convenient, but buying produce a couple of times a week is your best bet.** Ask the produce manager which vegetables are freshest, and lean on locally grown items, which have a shorter transit time. Of course, if you happen to find yourself with a slightly tired-looking bunch of spinach, don't toss it. Just cook it in a skillet with some olive oil and finish wilting it. (But don't boil it. See page 61.) It's still a good nutrition deal.

YOU ALWAYS CHOOSE FRESH
over canned or frozen.

In this case, fresh (left) beats frozen (right).

THE RESULT

You're missing out on convenient options.

THE FIX

You can't beat the flavor of fresh, seasonal produce, but on those days when you don't have time to prep, canned or frozen are convenient options. Frozen fruits and vegetables are flash-frozen within hours of harvesting, which means that, nutritionally, they're almost identical to fresh and are sometimes better. This assumes you don't buy frozen varieties that have syrups or seasonings as part of the mix, which can contain added sugar and sodium. Minimal (or no) prep is required, and you can pour them directly from the bag into soups or batters. One caveat: Fresh produce (like strawberries) often trumps frozen and canned in a beauty contest. Opt for fresh when appearance is crucial.

YOU WASH AND STORE ALL YOUR PRODUCE
when you get home from the grocery store.

THE RESULT

Mushy fruits and vegetables

Squish

Pretty and plump

THE FIX

When dealing with fresh fruits and vegetables, it's best to wash them when you need them. Why? Water accelerates deterioration, particularly in more fragile items like berries. If you wash your beautiful produce early, it may turn into a mushy mess by the time you're ready to use it.

IN YOUR DAILY CALORIE COUNT
you consider fruits like bananas and apples free.

THE RESULT

You're eating better but may be taking in more calories than you think.

THE FIX

Nothing with calories is really free. We're not knocking fruit—a nutrient-rich banana has only about 105 calories, and an ounce of baked chips has about 120, so swapping one for the other is a good nutrition deal.

But simply *adding* fruit will, in the long run, add up calorie-wise. **Focus more on healthy choices and less on calories, but be mindful that no food is free.**

YOU'RE ON A VEGGIE KICK,
boiling lots every night.

THE RESULT

Vitamin-rich pot water

THE FIX

Dropping foods that are rich in water-soluble vitamins (the Bs, including folate, and vitamin C) into cooking water leaches out some of their goodness. That's fine for a soup or stew, but less so if you're draining the vegetables. A Danish study found that boiled broccoli retained only 45% to 64% of its vitamin C after 5 minutes of boiling; steamed broccoli kept 83% to 100%. **So haul out the steamer. Microwaving is also a good option.**

YOUR TOMATOES
aren't quite ripe.

THE RESULT

Blah flavor

Not quite there yet

THE FIX

It happens. You choose tomatoes that just aren't ready. **One way to speed up the ripening process is to place the fruit in a brown paper bag and let it sit.** Check every day to see if it's reached the perfect shade of ripeness. Ripe tomatoes should still be slightly firm and smell like a tomato, particularly at the stem end.

YOU REFRIGERATE
tomatoes.

> ### THE RESULT
>
> Mushy, mealy texture

Blame the fridge for the mealiness. Bleh!

THE FIX

The refrigerator is no place for fresh tomatoes. Temperatures below about 55° damage their flavor, although some flavor may come back if the tomato is allowed to return to room temperature for a day or two before it's eaten. However, the texture will be irrevocably damaged, and you'll be left with an unfortunate collection of soft, mealy tomatoes. **For the best flavor, store them on the counter.** Cut tomatoes spoil quickly if not refrigerated, so, when possible, eat the whole fruit.

YOU REFRIGERATE WATERMELONS
as soon as you buy them.

THE RESULT

Less lycopene

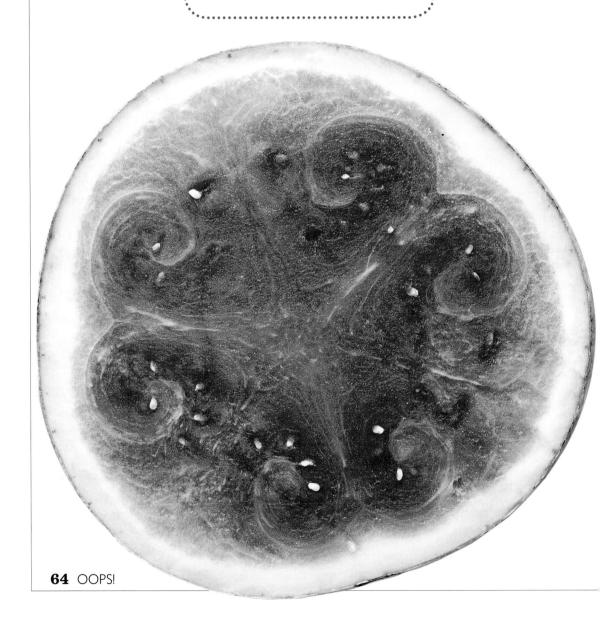

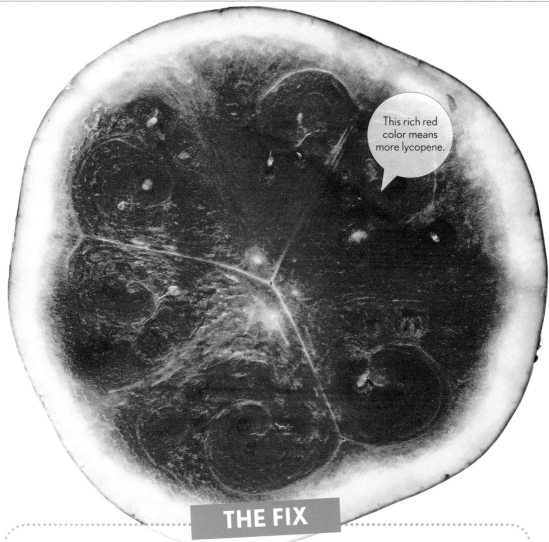

This rich red color means more lycopene.

THE FIX

Temperature affects the development and availability of lycopene, an antioxidant that gives watermelon, tomatoes, guavas, and red-fleshed grapefruits their rich red color. The USDA Agricultural Research Service found that after two weeks, melons stored at room temperature developed a richer rouge and gained as much as 40% more lycopene (14mg per 1½ cups), depending on the variety, than melons stored in the refrigerator—that's nearly half of an acceptable daily intake of 30mg. **To get the maximum benefit, let whole watermelons sit on the counter for up to five days to fully ripen and develop lycopene, and then place them in the fridge to chill.** If the melon has been cut, it should be refrigerated immediately.

YOUR LEMON (OR LIME)
isn't producing much juice.

Avoid those plastic lemon-shaped containers of juice. They do contain lemon juice, but the taste is noticeably off—not fresh, a bit harsh and thin.

THE RESULT

Less of that lively flavor you're craving

THE FIX

Before juicing a room-temperature lemon, lime, or other citrus fruit, use the palm of your hand to roll it on the countertop to break down the cells that hold liquid.

If a fruit is especially hard (and sometimes it's difficult to find a good one in an entire supermarket bin), microwave it for 20 seconds. You should get 2 to 3 tablespoons of juice per fruit.

YOU ZEST
with too much zest.

THE RESULT

Bitterness

This is bitter!

THE FIX

Grated fresh citrus rind adds wonderful, tangy flavor to a variety of dishes, but if you zest until you reach the white part of the skin, and then zest some more, your dish will suffer from your exuberance. **The white membrane (pith) is very bitter and those tiny grated pieces can be tedious, if not impossible, to remove.**

YOU FREEZE FRESH FRUIT
in zip-top freezer bags.

THE RESULT

Thawed berries that are
a mushy mess

THE FIX

Freezing fresh fruit lets you preserve a delightful dose of summer flavor even months after the season has passed. But if your fruit emerges from the thaw in a squishy clump with juice spilling out, it's barely fit for smoothies. The freezing method is the culprit: If you're putting raspberries, blueberries, peaches, and the like in bags to freeze, you're doing it wrong.

The longer it takes food to freeze, the larger the ice crystals will be. These big chunks of ice destroy cell walls inside the food, which destroys the structural integrity of the fruit when it thaws. Food freezes faster if there's cold air circulating around it. **Spread fruit pieces in an even layer on a baking sheet, making sure none are touching, and place the sheet in the back of your freezer.** Once items are frozen, transfer them to a zip-top freezer bag for freezer storage.

YOU GET YOUR IRON
mainly from spinach.

THE RESULT

You may get lots of nutrients—but not much iron.

THE FIX

Iron is important for energy because it helps deliver oxygen to every cell in your body, but it can be tricky to get from non-meat sources. Spinach and other plant sources are rich in what is called non-heme iron. Only about 2% to 20% of non-heme iron is absorbed, versus 15% to 35% of the heme iron found only in animal foods, specifically meat. **Vitamin C helps increase your absorption of non-heme iron, so pair iron-fortified breakfast cereal with a glass of OJ, or add grapefruit segments to your spinach salad.**

YOU DON'T BABY your greens.

THE RESULT

Your lettuce is lifeless.

This one stayed perky.

Drab and sad

THE FIX

Nice lettuce is a mighty pretty thing until it shrivels and withers—or, worse, rots and blackens around the edges. Once opened, even relatively shelf-stable bagged lettuces suffer this fate. The main storage problem is usually too much moisture, but lettuce needs *some* water to stay crisp; otherwise leaves dry out and droop. **The key is keeping lettuce moist, but just barely.** Loosely wrap the lettuce (including bagged lettuces) in slightly damp paper towels, and seal in a zip-top bag. This will absorb excess water without dehydrating the leaves. Store in your crisper drawer—the best spot for consistent controlled humidity—and don't wash lettuce until you're ready to use it.

YOU SERVE ALL YOUR GUAC
at once.

THE RESULT

Icky, khaki-colored dip

Si, señor!

THE FIX

Guacamole is a surefire party pleaser, at least for those who arrive early. Stragglers know they're late when the dip has been overtaken by a muddy brown shade. Obviously, oxygen is the enemy of guac, and leaving the pit in the dip (an old myth) doesn't help. **To delay the oxidation process, the antioxidant properties of ascorbic acid in lemon and lime juice are your first line of defense.** Toss cubed avocado in citrus juice, about 3 tablespoons per avocado, and then drain before mashing, reserving the juice. After mashing all your ingredients, add some of the juice back to taste. **Your dip will still brown eventually if you serve it all at once,** so dole it out in small batches, with the rest stored in the fridge like so: Rub a little olive oil onto a sheet of plastic wrap; then press the wrap, oil side down, onto the surface of the dip. The thin film of oil creates an impermeable barrier, with the plastic as a reliable backup.

THE RECIPE CALLS FOR MINCED GARLIC—
you stop at coarsely chopped.

You stink.

THE RESULT

Fewer heart-healthy compounds in your Caesar salad

It's the thiosulfinates.

THE FIX

Minced garlic is more redolent than chopped because the pungent, heart-healthy thiosulfinates are created as the clove is cut, so more cutting means more of these compounds. Thiosulfinates prevent blood platelets from clumping, which helps keep arteries unobstructed. One study showed that whole garlic had no significant effect on platelets compared to garlic put through a press. Grate garlic on a microplane, and you'll release even more.

YOU CHOP TONS OF GARLIC,
and then your hands reek all day.

THE RESULT

Vampires stay away—and so does everyone else.

THE FIX

To lift the smell, **wash your hands with soap and water, and then rub them on stainless steel.** A skillet, faucet, or fork will work as long as it's stainless steel. Wash with soap and water again.

YOU ADD GARLIC TO
your sauté too early.

THE RESULT

Bitter and burned bits

Time to start over.

THE FIX

Cooking garlic mellows the flavor and pungency, but if you cook it too long or over heat that's too high (or both), you're left with a pan full of bitter, burned bits. Garlic is more delicate than, say, onion because it contains less water, which makes it brown more quickly and dry out faster. To prevent this (there's no way to salvage a dish with burned garlic in the mix), **sauté the garlic first, and then remove it before adding meats or vegetables that require longer cooking times.** Or add the garlic toward the end of cooking.

YOU CUT ONIONS
with a dull knife.

THE RESULT

You shed more tears.

I don't want to make you cry.

THE FIX

Dull knives break more of the onion's cells, releasing more of the sulfuric compounds that bring tears to your eyes. One way to minimize eye irritation (without donning safety goggles) is to **use a sharp knife, which reduces the amount of tear-inducing compounds that are crushed. Also, work fast, and attack the root end last—it has the highest sulfur concentration.** You can also chill the onions in the fridge for 10 to 15 minutes before chopping to help reduce the noxious output.

YOU TRY TO RUSH
caramelizing onions.

Sautéed onions—good but not great

THE RESULT

Your onions are a far cry from the melt-in-your-mouth caramelized ideal.

Caramelized perfection

THE FIX

If you want true, sweet, creamy caramelized onions to top your burger or pizza, you need to cook them over medium-low to low heat for a long time, maybe up to an hour. If you crank up the heat and try to speed up the process, you'll get a different product—onions that may be crisp-tender and nicely browned but lack that characteristic translucence and meltingly tender quality you want. Bottom line: Know that caramelized onions take time, and plan to cook them when you can give them the time they need.

YOUR BRUSSELS SPROUTS
are bitter.

THE RESULT

Off-putting flavor that makes
you rethink sprouts

The bitter end

THE FIX

The compounds that give Brussels sprouts their bitterness are concentrated in the center stem of the sprout, so **it helps to halve or finely slice the sprouts before cooking.** The exposure to heat at the site where these compounds congregate helps subdue the bitter flavor. Boiling helps leach out some of the bitterness, but if you prefer a crisper texture, sauté in a skillet with a bit of sugar (brown sugar or maple syrup works fine, too); cook just until tender. The sugar caramelizes, counteracting some of the bitter flavors. You can also roast or sauté the Brussels sprouts with other strong flavors, like garlic and red chile flakes, and fat (olive oil or bacon) to soften the flavor. If all else fails, you can remove the center stem altogether.

YOU FORGO GLOVES
when working with hot peppers.

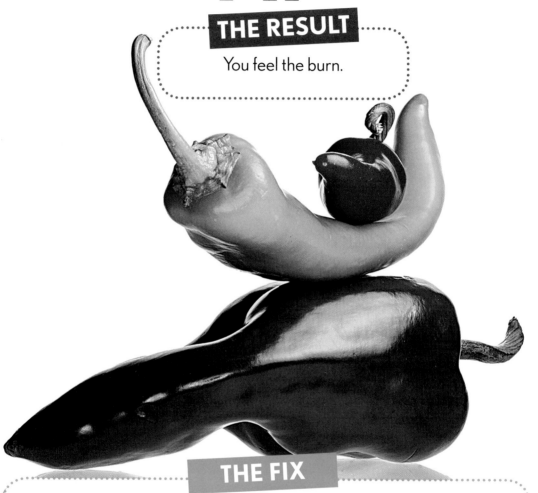

THE RESULT

You feel the burn.

THE FIX

Wear gloves while working with fiery chile peppers or you might find your skin burning. Capsaicin, the compound that gives peppers their kick, sticks to your hands and gloves, so be mindful of the things you touch while working with them. The compound spreads easily to any part of your skin that your capsaicin-covered hands touch, including your eyes. Ouch!

TO TAME THE HEAT,
you ditch only the seeds.

THE RESULT

You may still feel some heat.

THE FIX

Remember the membranes.
That white part contains the same burn-inducing compound, capsaicin, that's found in the seeds and can leave your skin red and tingling.

I'm pretty hot.

CHILE HEAT INDEX

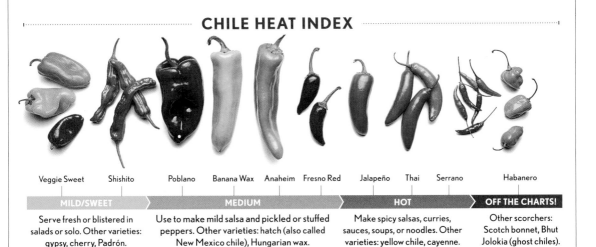

Veggie Sweet	Shishito	Poblano	Banana Wax	Anaheim	Fresno Red	Jalapeño	Thai	Serrano	Habanero

MILD/SWEET	MEDIUM	HOT	OFF THE CHARTS!
Serve fresh or blistered in salads or solo. Other varieties: gypsy, cherry, Padrón.	Use to make mild salsa and pickled or stuffed peppers. Other varieties: hatch (also called New Mexico chile), Hungarian wax.	Make spicy salsas, curries, sauces, soups, or noodles. Other varieties: yellow chile, cayenne.	Other scorchers: Scotch bonnet, Bhut Jolokia (ghost chiles).

YOU DON'T GIVE YOUR BEANS
an ice bath.

THE RESULT

Green beans that aren't
that green

Be kind to chlorophyll, the delicate source of the green.

THE FIX

When vegetables take a sad turn from bright green to khaki drab, it conjures memories of grade-school cafeteria food and the ruined texture of canned asparagus. **The most common culprits: overcooking and acidic dressings.** Vegetables such as green beans, broccoli, and asparagus lose their bright color and crisp texture after 6 or 7 minutes of cooking. If you know you'll be eating them immediately, just remove, drain, and serve. But if you'll be busy assembling other dishes, consider blanching and shocking: Cook for 2 minutes in salted boiling water, and then remove the vegetables and immediately plunge them into ice water. The ice bath halts the cooking process and helps set the color. Later, the chilled vegetables can be quickly reheated—by sautéing, for instance—without losing their green. But blanching won't help if you dress them too soon with an acid, such as vinegar or lemon juice. Wait until just before serving.

YOU DROWN
your greens.

THE RESULT

Your salad goes limp.

THE FIX

Tender greens like Boston lettuce, mâche, and arugula are delicate little things that perish at the mere rumor of mistreatment (tearing or roughly handling lettuce bruises it), but even crisp, hearty lettuces like romaine need to be handled with care. **Dress your greens just before serving, particularly when using a vinaigrette: Oil quickly permeates the waxy surface of leafy greens, turning them dark and droopy.** If you've washed your greens, use a salad spinner or blot them delicately with paper towels to dry them. Water clinging to leaves will repel oil-based vinaigrettes and thin out creamy dressings, leading to bland salad.

How you add the dressing also matters: Put dry greens in a bowl, and pour the dressing down the sides of the bowl, not onto the greens—you'll dress them more evenly this way. Use less dressing than you think you'll need (to avoid overdressing). Gently toss, adding dressing as needed, until the greens are lightly coated. If you do overdress them, a quick whirl in the salad spinner will shake off any excess.

YOU STORE FRESH HERBS
improperly.

THE RESULT

Wilty herbs

What a waste!

THE FIX

To keep your fresh herbs fresh, place them in a glass filled with water, as you would a flower arrangement. Put a plastic bag over the leaves, and store in the refrigerator. Change the water every other day. You can also wrap the stems in damp paper towels and store in a zip-top plastic bag. Both methods keep your herbs fresher longer.

YOU IGNORE YOUR POTATOES
after cutting them.

THE RESULT

Brown potatoes

THE FIX

It's not a pretty sight when the white flesh of potatoes turns brown after you've cut or peeled them. **To prevent the flesh from oxidizing, fill a large bowl with enough water to cover the potatoes. After cutting or peeling, immediately place the potatoes into the bowl of water, and then immediately drain.** The longer the potatoes sit in the water, the more starch will be removed—just 5 minutes in the water can cause the potatoes to dry out. That's a good thing when making oven fries, but not if you want a moister potato.

YOUR OVEN FRIES
fizzle.

THE RESULT

Potatoes that are pale and soggy or burned (or both!)

THE FIX

It seems counterintuitive, but for perfect comfort fries, give the spuds a bath. Nearly half a potato's weight is accounted for by water. Soaking pulls out starch, which reduces the water content of the potatoes: less water, less steaming in the oven. Start with baking (russet) potatoes; they're drier than waxy varieties. Cut each peeled potato in half lengthwise, halve again, and slice each quarter into ¼-inch-thick strips (using a mandoline is nice, but not essential). Even thickness and wide surface area prevent burning and give you more crispy real estate. Soak potatoes in cold water for 30 minutes, and then dry thoroughly with a paper towel. Toss with olive oil, and spread on a parchment paper–lined baking sheet. Don't overcrowd the fries or they'll end up soggy. Bake on the bottom rack at 400° for 35 minutes. Flip once halfway through.

YOU RUSH YOUR
baked potatoes.

THE RESULT

Hard spots in the middle

Eat the skin. It adds vitamin C and nearly 5 grams of fiber.

THE FIX

Our guaranteed-great method for a perfect baked potato: Rub a russet potato with olive oil and kosher salt, and bake at 375° for an hour or until soft to the touch. Don't wrap it in foil; the skin won't crisp. Place a baking sheet on the rack below the potatoes to catch any oil or salt that drips. If you're short on time, cut a slit in the top of each potato to let steam escape, and microwave for 9 minutes. But be aware, microwaved potatoes won't cook as evenly and can have a coarse, grainy texture.

YOU MAKE MASHED POTATOES
in the mixer.

THE RESULT

Gluey potatoes destined
for the trash

THE FIX

Overcooked or insufficiently drained potatoes can become sticky, as can the wrong kind of potato, but the main problem is overworked spuds. The science is simple: Boiled potatoes develop swollen starch cells. When ruptured during mashing, the cells release starch. The more cells ruptured, the gummier the mashed potatoes. **If you use an electric mixer or food processor to mash your potatoes, you'll probably beat them mercilessly and end up with wallpaper paste.** Instead, use a potato masher, or even better, pass the potatoes through a ricer or food mill—which is gentler on the starch cells and will help prevent lumps—before mixing them with butter and hot milk.

Low-starch, waxy potatoes hold their shape well after boiling, so they require more effort to mash, which means you're more likely to overwork them. Try mashing them partway. High-starch baking potatoes (russets) break down more readily, yielding a light and fluffy mash—or, with a little more milk and butter, a smooth and creamy one.

YOU DICE POTATOES FOR POTATO SALAD AND THEN DROP THEM
into boiling water to cook.

THE RESULT

Mushy texture

Potato salad perfection

THE FIX

To prevent mushiness, cut potatoes to uniform shapes and sizes, so they'll cook evenly. If they're different sizes, some will become overcooked and mushy while others will still have an undesirable crunch. Waxy, low-starch potatoes, like red potatoes, work best in potato salads because when cooked properly, they don't become mushy. **Also, when cooking your potatoes, place them in cold water, and then bring to a boil.** This works to solidify the surfaces and helps prevent the pieces from getting too soft as the interior cooks, so they hold their shape nicely in a potato salad.

YOU CHOOSE PRODUCTS "MADE WITH WHOLE GRAINS" to up your whole-grain intake.

THE RESULT

You may not be getting all the whole grains you think you are.

THE FIX

When this phrase appears on a package, it doesn't mean "made *exclusively* with whole grains." No regulations govern the specific percentage, so while the product will contain some whole grains, the rest of the ingredients could include refined flour, which offers significantly fewer nutritional benefits—less fiber and nutrients. The Whole Grain Stamp requires at least 8g of whole grains per serving, so it's a good guide. Look for it on packages to help you get closer to the daily goal of 48 grams.

YOU CHOOSE BRAN CEREAL
because it's high in fiber.

THE RESULT

You miss out
on whole grains.

THE FIX

Don't confuse whole grains with fiber. **Bran cereal may have more fiber than a whole-grain flake cereal (because it contains only the wheat's fiber-loaded bran), but it won't necessarily have the nutritional benefits that other whole-grain cereals offer.** For a processed food, cereal, bread, or pilaf to be considered whole grain, the product must contain all three whole-grain components: the germ, the endosperm, and the bran. The bran is full of fiber, while the germ and endosperm have many of the phytonutrients (beneficial chemicals found in plant foods), antioxidants, and other compounds believed to contribute to whole grains' multiple health benefits.

YOU DO A FREEHAND POUR OF CEREAL
at the breakfast table.

THE RESULT

You're likely to eat enough
for 1.4 people.

Actual Average
Most people poured:
$1^2/_5$ cups = 168 calories

Recommended
How much Special K the box suggests:
1 cup = 120 calories

Don't use a large cereal bowl—it makes a smart portion look paltry.

THE FIX

When we asked 100 people to show us their typical cereal pour, only 1 in 10 poured close to the recommended portions. For flake cereals, the average pour was 40% more than the 1-cup serving size. A full cup of fat-free milk in the bowl means you've added 40 more calories over the label standard. Breakfast requires lots of little portion decisions, all made when potentially groggy: OJ, coffee cream, jam for toast. **What to do: Read labels, and then practice with a measuring cup, just to get an idea of the recommended serving. If you change cereals, start over.**

Biggest Pour
$3^2/_3$ cups = 440 calories

YOU ONLY EAT HOT CEREAL ON THE WEEKEND
when you can slow-cook some steel-cut oats.

THE RESULT

You bypass one of the easiest ways to get whole-grain, fiber-rich goodness.

THE FIX

Turns out an oat is an oat, whether it's steel cut from the original groat or rolled flat and even presteamed so it will cook in 90 seconds. **Flattening and steaming doesn't remove whole-grain benefits, so you get all of the vitamins, minerals, antioxidants, and oaty fiber.** Yes, the steel-cut variety is nutty, chewy, and delicious, but instant is so darned weekday convenient. The key: Embrace all oats. One caveat: Prepackaged flavored oats can contain added sugar and salt.

YOU CUT BAKERY BREAD
using the closest knife within reach.

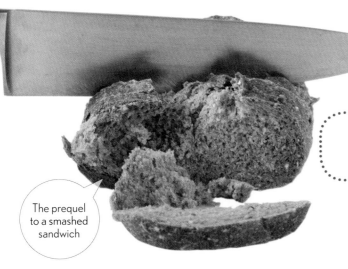

The prequel to a smashed sandwich

THE RESULT

Your loaf ends up flat.

THE FIX

Use a serrated knife. Those small, scalloped grooves in the blade are ideal for cutting through foods with a hard exterior and softer interior, like bread, without squashing it. The reason it works so well: Like a saw, the teeth of the blade catch and then rip as the knife smoothly slides through the food. It cuts cleanly and neatly through the crust, causing less splintering and flaking.

YOU REFRIGERATE YOUR BREAD
to make it last longer.

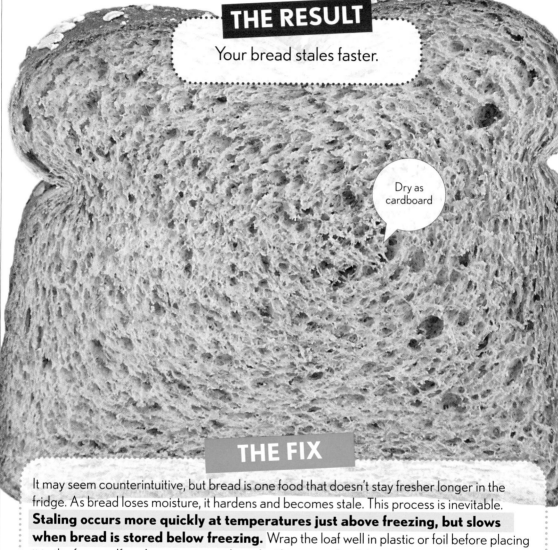

THE RESULT

Your bread stales faster.

Dry as cardboard

THE FIX

It may seem counterintuitive, but bread is one food that doesn't stay fresher longer in the fridge. As bread loses moisture, it hardens and becomes stale. This process is inevitable. **Staling occurs more quickly at temperatures just above freezing, but slows when bread is stored below freezing.** Wrap the loaf well in plastic or foil before placing it in the freezer. If you're going to use bread within a couple of days, then store it at room temperature. The bread will last a little longer if you transfer it to a zip-top plastic bag or other airtight container rather than the bakery bags with twist ties that loaves normally come in.

YOU ALWAYS OPT FOR HIGH-FIBER BREAD OVER 100% whole wheat.

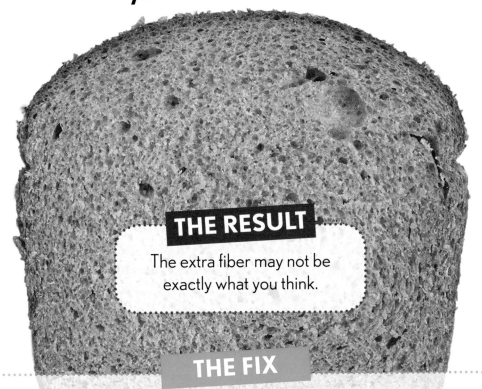

THE RESULT

The extra fiber may not be exactly what you think.

THE FIX

Many foods, not just breads, are boasting higher fiber content—even yogurt, which doesn't naturally contain fiber. The reason: Food manufacturers are isolating specific types of fiber and adding them to breads and other packaged foods. Can this added fiber take the place of whole grains and provide the same health benefits as naturally occurring fiber? The verdict is still out. Studies have found that these added fibers perform some of the same functions as dietary fiber, such as aiding in digestion and increasing satiety. They are not, however, equal to the fiber found naturally in food. It's difficult to compare a serving of nutrient-rich green beans to a packet of artificial sweetener with added fiber. **For the most part, foods with added fiber (or any other synthetically added nutrition enhancers, for that matter) don't provide the vitamins, minerals, and other nutrients associated with naturally high-fiber foods.**

YOU DON'T WARM TORTILLAS
before filling them.

THE RESULT

Tortillas that split and fall apart

I hate
split ends.

THE FIX

Tortillas, particularly corn tortillas, can be fragile. **Warming makes them more pliable and less likely to break when filled.** Wrap four or so in a damp paper towel and microwave at HIGH for 20 seconds. Or you can cook them in a cast-iron skillet or grill pan over medium-high heat or cook them directly on a gas flame. Cook the tortillas for 5 seconds on each side to heat them through, then cover the stack with a kitchen towel and keep warm. Use tortillas immediately if you're making enchiladas, or wrap them in paper towels or foil if you're serving at the table for assemble-your-own fajitas or soft tacos. The heat and steam created inside the sealed packet will keep the tortillas warm.

YOU DON'T GIVE
rice room to cook.

THE RESULT

Gummy rice

THE FIX

Slightly undercooked rice can sometimes be fixed with more water and time, but the dreaded gummy rice is destined for the trash. When rice is cooked in the traditional way—simmered in a 2:1 water-to-rice ratio in a lidded pot—the close-packed grains rub together and release starch, often leading to stickiness. **The solution is blessedly ratio-free, though it may seem counterintuitive: Use more water.** Lots more, so you cook the rice like pasta until it reaches the proper consistency, and then drain. The pasta method keeps rice from rubbing together too much as it cooks; draining ensures it won't suck up more water than it needs.

Nice rice!

YOU DON'T STIR
risotto constantly.

THE RESULT

The texture of your risotto isn't quite right.

Didn't get enough attention

THE FIX

The brilliance of this dish begins with the rice. You need a medium-grain rice, which absorbs more liquid than long-grain rice but won't become sticky like short-grain rice. The most common varieties are Arborio, Carnaroli, and Vialone Nano.

The looser variety

On the thick side

THE FIX (CONTINUED)

Constant stirring is key—the rice cooks more evenly and gains a creamier texture. The creamy texture is also a result of the gradual addition of hot liquid. Make sure your cooking liquid is hot, and incorporate it a half cup or so at a time, waiting until it's nearly absorbed before adding more.

Serve risotto immediately once it's reached the desired consistency and the rice is al dente: tender on the outside, slightly firm (but not crunchy) in the middle. The precise texture is difficult to control since the rice keeps absorbing liquid even after you're finished stirring, leaving a thick, gloppy mass. Set aside 2 tablespoons extra liquid (for a risotto that serves four) to stir in after pulling the risotto off the heat. It'll loosen the grains to ensure the dish stays creamy.

YOU COOK PASTA IN A
skimpy amount of water.

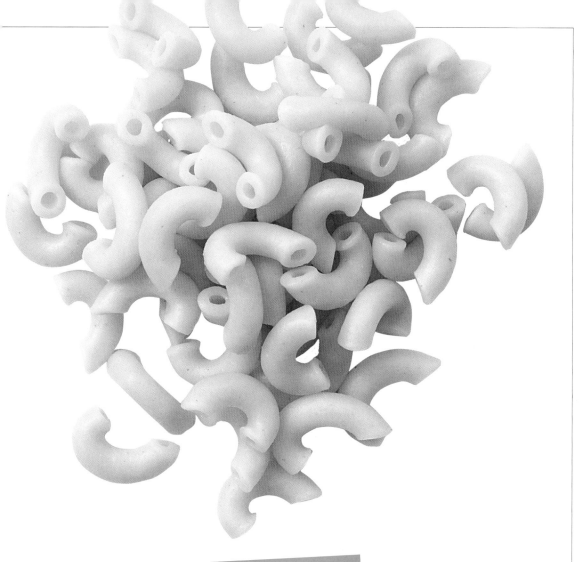

THE FIX

To get the best results, give the pasta some space. **Fill a Dutch oven or stockpot with 5 quarts of water for each pound of pasta.** This water-to-pasta ratio gives the pasta plenty of room to move around, allowing each piece to absorb the same amount of water for even cooking and minimal, if any, clumping. If the pieces are too close to one another, they absorb the minimal amount of water separating them, and then their slightly softer surfaces gel together. Make sure you bring the water to a rolling boil before adding the pasta, then give the pasta a stir to prevent it from sticking to itself or the bottom of the pan. Begin timing when the water returns to a boil.

Charred

OOPS!

DAIRY, EGGS, SEAFOOD, POULTRY & MEATS

YOU DON'T SHAKE SOY MILK
before drinking it.

THE RESULT

You're not getting as much calcium as you think.

THE FIX

Calcium added to soy milk is good for bones. But it tends to settle at the bottom of the carton, and then can be quite tough to redistribute into the milk. According to a study from Creighton University in Nebraska, **fortified soy milks may deliver only 25% to 79% of the promised calcium, depending on the type used and the way it's added. In cow's milk, by contrast, calcium is naturally suspended throughout the liquid.** To avoid tossing the good stuff out, shake, shake, shake that soy milk *before each pour.* And consume calcium from a variety of sources to get the full amount you need daily: 1,000 to 1,200mg.

YOU SWITCH TO ALMOND MILK
to save calories and fat.

THE RESULT

Less calcium and less protein

THE FIX

Almond milk has a nutty, toasty flavor with a faint bitter background. It's made from ground almonds that are mixed with water, and then fortified with nutrients and thickened with agents like lecithin and carrageenan for body. **At 60 calories per cup, it has fewer calories than fat-free milk, but it also has less protein (1.1g) and calcium (7mg) compared to the 8.3g of protein and more than 300mg of calcium in each cup of milk.** If you make the switch, be sure to find other sources of these nutrients or try another milk substitute.

YOU PICK BROWN EGGS
over white.

I'm special.

THE RESULT

You pay up to a 25% price premium for what is, basically, an aesthetic choice.

Not really

THE FIX

Even in the era of fancy omega-3 eggs, brown eggs retain a certain rustic allure. **But a large brown egg contains the exact same proportion of white and yolk, and the same nutrients, as a white egg.** Brown eggs simply come from a different breed of hens, which are often bigger birds and require more feed than standard white-egg-laying Leghorns. Those costs are usually passed on, adding to the perceived specialness of brown eggs. Instead, choose by wallet or style sensibility; either way, you'll pick a good egg.

YOUR EGG SEPARATION
is a bit careless.

THE RESULT

Whites that don't whip properly

Tainted

THE FIX

Whipped egg whites are used in meringues, some cakes, and other baked goods. To get the best results, the whites must be pristine. Even one speck of yolk will prevent them from whipping to their maximum volume. (See page 233 for more information.) To separate the two, here's a method that produces clean results: Crack the egg. **Hold a cupped hand over one bowl. With the other, gently separate the shell along the crack, letting the yolk and whites fall into your waiting hand. Keeping the solid yolk in your hand, allow the whites to drip through your fingers into the bowl below.** Place the yolk in a second bowl, and throw away the shell. Inspect the whites to make sure none of the yolk or shell made it into the bowl. If so, remove those bits. Stored in an airtight container, egg whites will keep in the fridge for up to four days, and yolks for two days.

YOU BOIL YOUR
poached eggs.

THE RESULT

Ugly, unappetizing eggs

Stringy

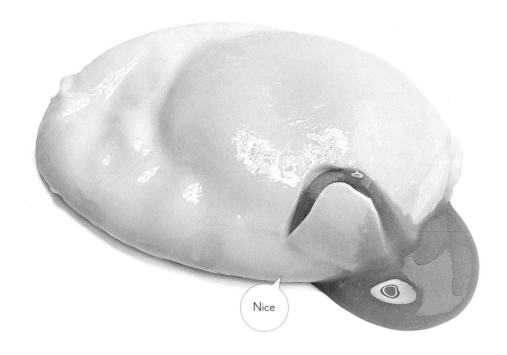

Nice

THE FIX

The typical botched poached egg is tentacled, scary, tough, overcooked. How can such a simple food confound so many cooks? Advice abounds on the process, but here's what we've found works best: Fill a wide saucepan or sauté pan with about 2 inches of water. **Bring it to a gentle simmer—not a rolling boil, which toughens and twists the whites. Add a few teaspoons of vinegar, which helps eggs keep their shape.** Crack eggs (fresher are better since they won't spread as much) into small ramekins or custard cups. The cups let you gently pour the eggs into the pan so the whites stay in a tight circle, and they ensure that you won't crack a broken-yolk dud into the water. Cook 3 minutes (the whites should be set and the yolks still creamy), and then remove carefully with a slotted spoon. Drain them for a few seconds, or blot with a paper towel. Voilà: No more poor poaching.

WHEN MAKING HARD-COOKED EGGS,
you boil them—hard.

THE RESULT

Icky eggs

We've all followed someone's can't-fail advice for preparing hard-cooked eggs, then puzzled over less-than-perfect results: eggs with rubbery whites, chalky yolks, and that telltale green-gray film between yolk and white. The cause? Temperature differential: The white of an egg dropped into boiling water cooks much faster than the yolk at the center, and that's trouble. By the time the yolk sets, the white is tough. And if the egg stays over high heat too long or isn't cooled quickly after cooking, sulfur in the white will react with the iron in the yolk, creating that nasty off-colored ring.

Here's the fix: To keep the temperature of the white and yolk close, heat the eggs gradually. Place them in a saucepan, cover them with an inch or two of cold water, and set the pan over high heat. When the water reaches a full boil, remove from heat, cover the pan, and, for large eggs, let them stand for 10 minutes. (Timing will vary for medium or extra-large eggs.) This cooks them gently and keeps the whites from toughening. Peel the eggs immediately under cold running water or, if you're not using them right away, set them in an ice-water bath.

YOU SCRAMBLE EGGS over high heat.

Boing!

THE RESULT

Rubbery eggs

Soft and creamy

THE FIX

High heat is the enemy of scrambled eggs. If you enlist it in the quest for a quick breakfast, you'll inevitably end up with rubbery eggs. Instead, **heat a nonstick or cast-iron skillet over medium heat.** While the pan heats, whisk the eggs together just until the yolks are mixed with the whites. Pour the eggs into the pan, and let them cook for about a minute; then begin gently scraping the eggs with a spatula—scrape more often if you like smaller curds and less often if you like larger curds. Resist the urge to crank up the heat to finish them quickly. And just before you think they're done, take them off the heat. The eggs will continue to cook in the hot pan after they've been removed from the heat. You'll be left with creamy, soft, perfectly scrambled eggs.

YOU BUY EGGS FORTIFIED WITH OMEGA-3S
but only eat the whites.

THE RESULT

You miss out on the omega-3s.

THE FIX

Omega-3-fortified eggs come from chickens that have been fed a diet supplemented with omega-3 fatty acids (often from flaxseed), but **if you eat only the whites to save on fat and calories, you're missing out on those healthy fats and a host of other nutrients.** True, the yolk contains 1.6g of saturated fat, but it also has 2g of monounsaturated fat and 0.7g of polyunsaturated fat, plus folate, calcium, beta carotene, and iron.

YOU NEVER PRESS
tofu.

THE RESULT

Drab, flavorless tofu
without a sear

I could use some color.

Seared

THE FIX

Many varieties of tofu come packaged in water to keep them fresh. But, in order to get a beautiful, browned crust, some of the liquid will need to be pressed out so it won't release into the pan while the tofu cooks. **Once pressed, the tofu acts like a wrung-out sponge that's ready to soak up flavor from marinades and seasonings.** (You only need to press water-packed medium, firm, and extra-firm tofu, not the silken or soft varieties.) To press: Cut the block into even slices, and lay the slices on a few absorbent paper towels. Top with another layer of paper towels, and then place a heavy pan on top. Let stand for 30 minutes, pressing occasionally to release excess water.

YOU OVER-SALT
your soup.

THE RESULT

A potentially fixable mistake

THE FIX

The soup may be salvageable, depending on how much salt you added. **Here's the rescue plan: Cut a waxy potato (such as red or fingerling) into slices and add them to the pot; simmer 5 to 10 minutes, and then remove the potato slices with a slotted spoon.** The porous, low-sodium potatoes will have absorbed some of the salt. Taste the soup. If it's still too salty, dump it and start over.

YOU PUT A LARGE POT OF YOUR FAVORITE SOUP
in the fridge to cool.

THE RESULT

Potential for food-borne illness

THE FIX

A large amount of soup (or any food) in a large pot or container takes a long time to cool, and a chunk of that time will be in what food-safety experts refer to as the temperature danger zone: 40° to 140°, the optimal range for bacteria growth. **Instead of letting a large pot of soup cool on the stovetop or in the fridge, transfer the soup to smaller, shallow containers that allow it to cool more quickly.** And be sure to refrigerate it within two hours (or within one hour if the surrounding temperature is above 90°) to slow the growth of illness-causing bacteria.

YOU DON'T SKIM SOUP
because the fat adds flavor.

THE RESULT

Soup that sports
an oil slick

Greasy film

When a bowl of soup leaves lips as slick as if they'd just been slathered with balm, it's a bummer. This problem occurs most often with brothy, meaty soups, such as chicken noodle and beef barley. Fat from the meat—and from the oil or butter used to sauté the veggies—rises as the broth simmers. But even if you stand with a skimming spoon at the ready or try the messy and potentially scalding trick of dabbing the surface with a paper towel, you may still leave enough grease behind to annoy you. Instead, skim smarter. **Impurities and fat gather at the coolest spot, so move the soup pot halfway off the burner every 15 minutes or so, and skim from the edge that's off the heat.** Tilt the pan slightly as you skim to avoid removing too much broth. Simmer the soup gently, and never boil: That just churns the fat into the broth. If time allows, chill the soup overnight. Fat will solidfy on top; simply spoon it off before you reheat.

Beautiful broth

YOU BLEND HOT MIXTURES
in an enclosed blender.

THE RESULT

Soup on the ceiling

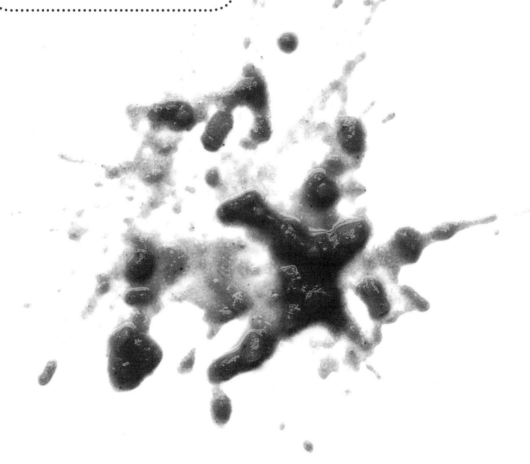

Skyrocketing soup (and the cleanup involved afterward) is most certainly not an ideal way to begin a meal. The reason for it: Steam (from the hot liquid) trapped in the confined space of the blender can create enough pressure to literally blow the top off. To prevent this, **remove the plastic center piece from the blender lid; this small hole will allow the steam to escape.** Then secure the lid on the blender. Place a clean towel over the opening in the blender lid (to prevent splatters and protect your hand from the heat), and blend. Also, be sure the blender is no more than two-thirds full. Blend in batches, if needed.

YOU USE FAT-FREE OR LOW-FAT CHEESE
to top casseroles.

THE RESULT

A plastic-like topping

Rubbery

THE FIX

Besides producing a difference in flavor, the lack of fat in fat-free cheese also alters its melting properties, producing plastic-like results. This difference isn't as obvious when cheese is stirred into a dish or used as a filling in tacos, but it becomes quite noticeable atop casseroles and enchiladas because the rubbery finish and texture is on full display. Instead, forgo fat-free and opt for a reduced-fat or even full-fat version. Like butter, moderate amounts of reduced-fat and full-fat cheese have a place in a healthy diet. **Fat-free cheese simply can't produce the delicious mouthfeel and melty texture that makes cheese so delicious.**

YOU AVOID SEAFOOD
because of the risk of mercury.

High in mercury

THE RESULT

You miss out on great health benefits.

Lower in mercury

The seafood over here is lowest in mercury.

THE FIX

Seafood contains too many healthy nutrients to cut it out of your diet completely. It's a source of high-quality, lean protein and is low in saturated fat—and fattier types of fish (like salmon, sardines, and anchovies) are rich in omega-3s. In fact, the USDA's Dietary Guidelines for Americans recommend two servings of seafood per week. Mercury can inhibit development of the brain and nervous system in fetuses and young children, so pregnant women, women who may become pregnant, nursing mothers, and young children should eat varieties that are lower in mercury. **While there are many low-mercury fish and shellfish in the sea, there are a handful of fish to avoid, including shark, swordfish, king mackerel, and tilefish.** Check local advisories about the safety of fish and shellfish caught in nearby lakes, rivers, bays, and coastal areas.

YOU ASSUME ALL CANNED TUNA
is equal nutritionally after draining.

THE RESULT

You may not get as many healthy fats.

THE FIX

Tuna varieties offer varying amounts of omega-3s. Albacore, a widely available species labeled "white meat tuna," has the most: 1.1g in a 4-ounce serving packed in water and 0.5g in the same amount packed in oil. Since omega-3s are oils, they don't disperse when the fish is packed in water, so these beneficial fatty acids remain in the fish when the water is drained. But when packed in oil, the fish's natural oils intermingle with the packing oil, so some of the omega-3s are lost when the fish is drained. **For maximum omega-3 benefits, choose tuna canned in water.** To make sure you're making a sustainable choice, buy canned tuna that has been troll- or pole-caught in U.S. waters.

YOU USE WAX PAPER
to steam fish.

THE RESULT

The paper burns, and the liquid leaks through.

Charred

THE FIX

Cooking *en papillote*—steaming small portions of food in a wrapper—is a classic technique that allows food to take on the character of the fresh herbs, broth, or seasonings surrounding it. **Parchment paper performs the best since it's sturdy, burn-resistant, and impervious to liquids. If you're out of parchment paper, substitute foil—not wax paper, which tears and burns too easily and will eventually leak.** Stick strictly to parchment paper for recipes containing a salt rub or highly acidic ingredients to avoid discoloration and off odors caused by a chemical reaction with the aluminum.

YOU BUY SCALLOPS
packed in liquid.

THE RESULT

Skimpy seared scallops

Meager

Plump

THE FIX

It's disappointing to see the beautiful, plump scallops you bought shrink when cooked. **The culprit here is the salt solution they were treated with and packaged in.** The scallops—often labeled "wet-packed"—absorb the mixture and plump up, but when you cook them, the liquid cooks out, leaving you with smaller scallops and a higher sodium content. Dry-packed scallops are not chemically treated and are preferable to wet-packed for price, sodium content, and because they sear better. If the label doesn't specify, be sure to ask.

YOU AVOID SHRIMP
to cut back on cholesterol.

THE RESULT

You miss out on a lean source of protein—and delicious meals.

THE FIX

While the current USDA Dietary Guidelines for Americans still recommend consuming less than 300mg of cholesterol per day (200mg for those at risk of heart disease), it's a bit of an anachronism—a holdover from the time when researchers believed the amount of cholesterol you ate had a direct correlation to the amount floating around in your bloodstream. Since then, **extensive research has shown that saturated fat and trans fat have a much stronger influence on raising total and LDL ("bad") cholesterol than cholesterol from food.** Keep a closer watch on those fats and feel free to enjoy shrimp to fulfill the USDA's recommendation of two servings of seafood each week.

YOU DON'T PAY ATTENTION
to the fine print on poultry labels.

THE RESULT

You may be getting more sodium than you realize.

Fresh Chicken Boneless • Skinless
BREAST with **RIB MEAT**
enhanced with up to 15% chicken broth, salt and carrageenan

KEEP REFRIGERATED • PRODUCT OF USA

NET WT. 26.4 OZ. (1.65 LBS.)

100% Natural
*No Artificial Ingredients **No Added Hormones
*Minimally Processed **No Added Steroids

Protein   Fat   Reduced
22g   3g   Sodium
                46% less than
                regular product

USDA A GRADE

INSPECTED U.S. DEPARTMENT OF AGRICULTURE

**FEDERAL REGULATIONS PROHIBIT THE USE OF ARTIFICIAL STIMULANTS OR HORMONES IN POULTRY.

This tiny type means more salt.

THE FIX

About one-third of the fresh chicken found in supermarket meat cases has been injected with a mix of water, salt, and other additives. This is done to make naturally lean poultry meat juicier and more tender. **A raw 4-ounce serving of what's called "enhanced" poultry can contain as much as 440mg of sodium—nearly one-fifth of the current 2,300mg daily allotment from a source you'd never suspect.** It's also 500% more sodium than is found naturally in chicken, yet USDA policies allow poultry companies to label their enhanced products "100% natural" or "all natural," even though they've been injected with ingredients in concentrations that do not naturally occur in chicken. (Like many foods, chicken contains trace amounts of sodium and other minerals.)

Processors are required to disclose the injections, but the print on the package can be small and inconspicuous. To know if you're buying enhanced chicken, squint at the fine print, which will say something like, "contains up to 15% chicken broth." You can also check the ingredient list and the nutrition facts label. If the chicken is truly natural, the sodium won't be higher than 70mg per serving.

YOU ALWAYS CHOOSE CHICKEN BREASTS OVER THIGHS
to save on calories.

THE RESULT

Not as much savings as you think

THE FIX

It's true that dark meat is more caloric and higher in sat fat than white, but if you always choose white over dark for the health benefits, take this into consideration: **A 4-ounce serving of roasted dark-meat chicken contains just 50 more calories and 2.2g more sat fat than an equal amount of white meat.** So you can stray from your fidelity to white meat and opt for the richer flavor of dark meat from time to time.

YOU RINSE
raw chicken.

THE RESULT

You could be spreading bacteria all over the kitchen.

THE FIX

Rinsing doesn't remove or decrease the bacteria on the poultry; it actually increases the risk of cross-contamination. **The bacteria in raw poultry (and meat) juices can spread to your sink, utensils, kitchen surfaces, and other food and can only be destroyed in food by cooking.** (For sinks and kitchen surfaces, you'll need disinfectant spray and a clean kitchen towel or paper towel to kill bacteria.) Poultry needs to be cooked to an internal temperature of 165° and checked with a meat thermometer in the innermost part of the meat. Be sure to store raw chicken on the lowest shelf of the refrigerator and wrap it in disposable plastic bags or zip-top bags to prevent juices from contaminating cooked food or fresh produce.

YOU PUT A WET CHICKEN (OR TURKEY)
in the oven to roast.

Limp

Crisp!

THE RESULT

Skin that isn't crispy

THE FIX

To get crispy, the skin has to start dry and stay dry during cooking. Pat the skin of the bird as dry as possible with paper towels. Getting some separation between the skin and the meat helps, too. Starting at the neck cavity, loosen skin from the breasts and drumsticks by inserting your fingers, and gently pushing between the skin and the meat. You can create an herb-butter mixture to rub over the flesh under the loosened skin and on the skin for added flavor. Any salt rubbed on the skin will also draw moisture to the surface, where it will evaporate in the heat of the oven, further encouraging a deliciously crisp skin, which you can enjoy without feeling guilty.

Nutritionally, there's good news, too. Fifty-five percent of the fat in the skin is heart-healthy monounsaturated. Each ounce of meat from a Thanksgiving turkey contains 3g of saturated fat—comparable to 1¼ teaspoons of butter. In other words, the skin is not a deal-breaker when you're considering indulging.

YOUR TURKEY-CARVING SKILLS
are for the birds.

THE RESULT

The beautiful bird becomes a hacked-up mess.

Crime scene

Picture perfect

THE FIX

Turkey carving is a culinary responsibility that requires elbow room and a large, stable cutting surface—usually not the dining room table. **The key to properly breaking down a bird is the order in which you do it.** (This is where many cooks go wrong—trying to slice meat directly off a big, hot bird.) Leg quarters come off first, then breast meat, with the tucked-under wings serving to stabilize as you cut. Set the big pieces on a cutting board where you can deal with them properly. Take the breast meat off the bone in one piece, and then slice crosswise, which ensures uniformity and allows for slightly thicker slices that are juicier and less fibrous than thin portions. Cut the thigh meat into large chunks. Be sure to save room on the platter for the legs, too.

YOU PUT ALL THE SALT IN THE
marinade or breading.

THE RESULT

Underseasoned fish, poultry, or meats

All the salt doesn't go here.

THE FIX

Healthy cooks try to keep sodium levels in check and allocate only a small amount of salt to a recipe—so they need to maximize the salt's impact. But a chicken that's marinating in, say, citrus juice and a teaspoon of salt will absorb only a tiny amount of the marinade. **When you toss out the marinade, you also toss out most of the salt and its seasoning effect.** It's better to use a little salt in the marinade, then sprinkle the majority directly on the chicken after it comes out of the marinade. The same goes for breaded items: If all the salt is in the panko coating for the fish fillets, and you discard half of that panko after dredging, half of the flavor goes with it. Instead, sprinkle salt directly on the fillets, and then coat them with the breading.

YOU USE BOTH HANDS
to dredge.

THE RESULT

A wet mess

THE FIX

Most recipes that call for pan-frying or oven-frying use a three-step approach for the breaded coating: The food is first dusted in flour to help all the other coatings cling, then dipped into an egg wash to help the main coating adhere, and finally dredged in the main, heavier coating, such as breadcrumbs or cornmeal. This mix of wet and dry has the potential to create a mess of your kitchen, the ingredients, and the dish. **To keep the procedure tidy, it's helpful to designate one of your hands as the dry hand for handling the food as it goes into the dry ingredients and the other as the wet hand for dipping food into the egg wash.** If you use the same hand for every step, you'll end up with a flour-egg-breadcrumb coating in the dish and stuck to your skin, and a less-than-perfect coating on the food.

YOU THAW MEATS
on the counter.

THE RESULT

Potential for food-borne illness

THE FIX

Food should never be thawed by leaving it at room temperature for more than two hours. **While the center of the food may still be frozen as it thaws on the counter, the outer layer could be in the temperature danger zone (40° to 140°), giving any bacteria in the food ample time and an ideal environment in which to multiply.**

The ideal thawing method: Store food overnight in the refrigerator, where it will remain at a constant temperature of 40° or lower. If you're in a bigger hurry, seal the food in a waterproof zip-top plastic bag and submerge it in cold tap water, changing the water every 30 minutes. Small packages of food like seafood or chicken breasts may thaw in an hour or less, while a 3- to 4-pound piece of meat may take two to three hours. For whole turkeys, estimate 30 minutes per pound. And there's always microwave thawing. Be sure to cook the food immediately after thawing in the microwave, since some portions may have started to cook, bringing it into the 40° to 140° zone.

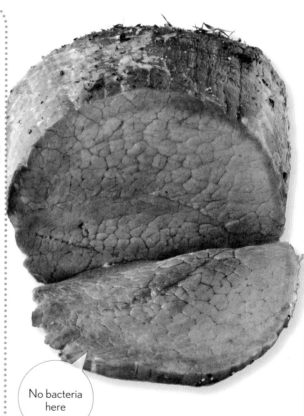

No bacteria here

YOU POP MEATS STRAIGHT FROM THE FRIDGE
into the oven or onto the grill.

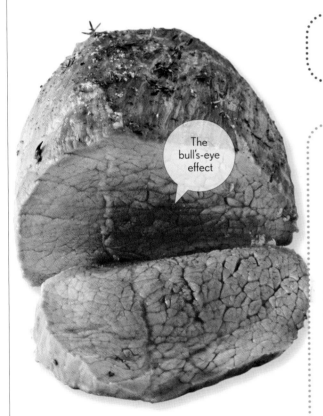

The bull's-eye effect

THE RESULT

Uneven cooking

THE FIX

Meats will cook much more evenly if you allow them to stand at room temperature for 15 to 30 minutes (depending on the size of the cut) to take the chill off. Putting a large roast into the oven refrigerator-cold will likely result in the outside being overcooked while the core struggles to get to a safe temperature. **As you slice the roast, you'll see a bull's-eye effect: The middle is rare (or even raw) while the outside is well done.** This is less of a problem with smaller cuts like chicken breasts—though even those benefit from resting at room temperature for 5 to 10 minutes before cooking.

YOU USE A SMALLER OR LARGER
slow cooker than the recipe calls for.

THE RESULT

Under- or overcooked food

Dried out and tough

THE FIX

It's important to use the size specified by the recipe to ensure proper cooking and safe temperatures. If you do try a different-sized cooker, make sure it's still between half and two-thirds full. If it's too full, the food will take too long to heat up, while underfilling the slow cooker will cause food, particularly meats, to dry out and become tough. The starting level of the food is the most important; it's fine if it cooks down. Be aware, however, that cooking times may vary—using a large slow cooker means the cook time may be less; if using a smaller one, the dish may need more time.

Keep ingredients refrigerated until ready to use. Because slow cookers don't heat food as quickly as conventional appliances, it's especially important not to allow perishables to sit out at room temperature, a prime environment for bacterial growth.

WHEN STIR-FRYING,
you don't cut food to the proper size.

THE RESULT

Some pieces are burned while others are undercooked.

The beauty of stir-frying is the short cook time—ideal for busy weeknight cooks. But if you're too lax when cutting, you may not get the dinner you'd hoped for. **When stir-frying, you need to cut food into pieces that are uniform in shape and size so they'll cook quickly in the high heat of your wok or skillet. If size varies widely, pieces will cook unevenly.**

It's ideal for most vegetables to be cut into thin, bite-sized pieces, especially those with high moisture content, such as summer squash and bell peppers. Denser vegetables like broccoli work well, too, but they may need to be blanched first or allowed to steam briefly with a little liquid after the initial stir-frying to become tender. Leafy greens cook in seconds once they hit the wok. Meats cut into thin, bite-sized strips cook beautifully.

YOU ADD COLD GROUND MEAT
to a hot pan.

THE RESULT

Dry meat

Destined
for dryness

THE FIX

Have you ever found meat swimming in juices shortly after you start cooking? The reason: **Adding cold meat to a hot pan cools the pan and may cause the meat to release the precious juices that keep it moist and flavorful.** To avoid the watered-out effect, let meat stand at room temperature for 15 to 30 minutes before cooking it, and make sure the pan is hot before adding the meat. And don't overcrowd the pan. If you're cooking more than one pound of meat, break it into batches, making sure to reheat the pan between batches.

YOU DON'T USE
a meat thermometer.

THE RESULT

Roast chicken, leg
of lamb, burgers, or beef
tenderloin turn out
over- or undercooked.

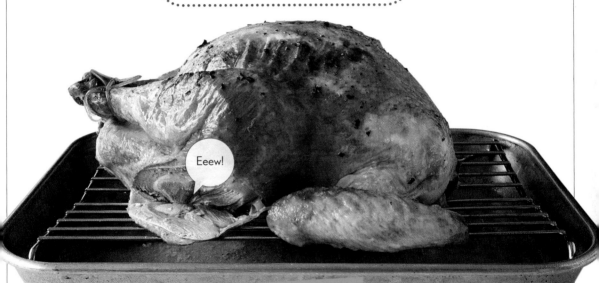

Eeew!

THE FIX

Small, inexpensive, and thoroughly unglamorous, the meat thermometer is one of the most valuable kitchen tools you can own. Appearances can deceive, but temperatures don't lie, so using one is the surest way to achieve a perfect roast chicken or beautiful medium-rare lamb roast. **We love digital probe thermometers, which allow you to set the device to the desired temperature.** A heat-proof wire leads to an external digital unit that sits outside the oven and beeps when the meat is ready. This speeds cooking by eliminating the need to open the oven door or grill lid to check the temp—which causes you to lose valuable heat.

YOU COOK PORK
until it's no longer pink.

THE RESULT

Overcooked meat

Perfectly pink

THE FIX

Pork with a bit of pink is indeed safe to eat. **The USDA recommends cooking pork to an internal temperature of 145° and letting it rest for 3 minutes after removing it from the grill or oven;** the temperature of the meat will continue to rise. (See opposite page for more on letting meat rest.) This temperature is standard for other red meats such as beef, veal, and lamb and is still higher than the temperature needed to kill pathogens. And better feeding and housing conditions for animals, along with safer production methods, have greatly decreased the risk of trichinosis, an illness long associated with pork. Use a thermometer placed in the thickest part of the meat to ensure it has reached the right temperature. Note: Ground meats must still be cooked to 160°.

YOU SLICE THE MEAT RIGHT
after cooking.

THE RESULT

Delicious juices vacate the
meat, leaving it dry.

THE FIX

Plan meals so that meat you roast, grill, sear, or sauté has time to rest at room temperature after it's pulled from the heat. That cooling-off time helps the juices, which migrate to the center of the meat, to be distributed more evenly throughout. The resting rule, by the way, applies equally to inexpensive skirt steak; premium, dry-aged, grass-fed steak; and poultry. **With small cuts like a steak or boneless, skinless chicken breast, 5 minutes is adequate.** A whole bird or standing rib roast requires 20 to 30 minutes. Tent the meat loosely with foil to keep it warm.

YOU DON'T BOIL THE MARINADE
before serving it with the meat.

THE RESULT

Potential for food-borne illness

THE FIX

Raw meat and marinades require some precautions. **If you're planning to serve the marinade as a sauce with the finished dish or to baste the meat or seafood with it, you must bring it to a boil and cook it for 5 minutes to kill any bacteria.** And always marinate meat and fish in the refrigerator in a nonreactive container— glass, ceramic, plastic, or stainless steel. Aluminum or copper containers can interact with acidic marinades, discoloring the food and giving it an unappetizing metallic taste.

YOU SLICE MEAT
with the grain.

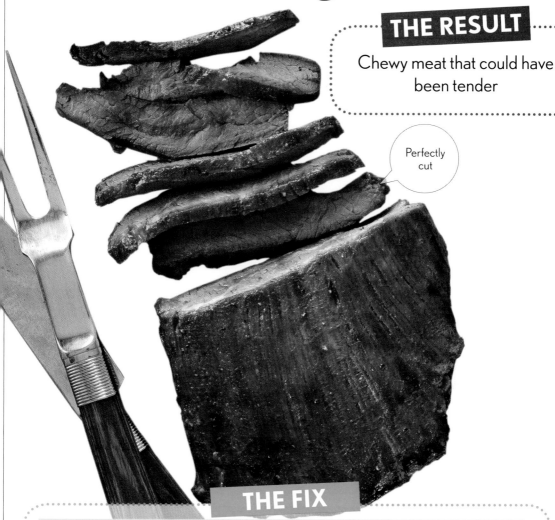

THE RESULT

Chewy meat that could have been tender

Perfectly cut

THE FIX

Cuts like flank steak and skirt steak come from harder-working muscles and generally have a tougher, larger grain (the muscle fibers). Cutting across the grain shortens those fibers, making the slices more tender and easier to chew. Look at the meat to determine the direction of the grain, and cut across rather than with it. This technique is particularly important for tougher cuts in which the grain is quite obvious, but it's also a good practice with more tender cuts like standing rib roast or even poultry.

YOU BUY 80/20 GROUND BEEF
because it's "lean."

THE RESULT

Way more fat in your burger or meat loaf than you thought

80% / 20%

THE FIX

The 80/20 ratio refers to the proportion of fat and protein in the grind, not the proportion of calories. Because fat contains more than twice the calories of protein (9 calories per gram versus 4), 20% of fat by weight contributes 72% of the total calories in a 3.5-ounce portion of raw ground beef, or about 180 of the 250 total calories. What to do: Buy a much leaner grind, such as 90/10, or ask for a lean whole cut, like sirloin or brisket, to be custom ground for you; it will be fresher anyway.

YOU SUB GROUND TURKEY
for lean ground beef to save on fat.

THE RESULT

Unless you're careful, not much savings

THE FIX

Turkey breast is lean, but dark meat isn't, and some ground turkey contains both, plus skin. A quarter-pound of regular ground turkey contains 3g saturated fat. Compare that to only 2.5g in the same amount of sirloin. Ground turkey breast, on the other hand, has just 0.5g sat fat, so the right cut of turkey is a significant fat-cutter. Read the label; buy lean.

YOU HANKER FOR SOME FAST FOOD.
Grilled chicken beats beef burger.

THE RESULT

Sodium city, and not necessarily much in the way of calorie savings either

THE FIX

Sodium can soar in a chicken sandwich for two reasons: First, the chicken breast may have been injected with a salty brine solution to help the meat stay moist. At Burger King, the Tendergrill Chicken Sandwich has 1,330mg sodium, and a majority of that comes from the chicken itself. (A Whopper Jr. burger has less than half the sodium, little of it from the beef, and 130 fewer calories.)

Second, lean chicken sometimes picks up salty passengers along the way, like the bacon and Swiss cheese on the McDonald's Premium Grilled Chicken Club sandwich. That baby has 1,030mg sodium. You have a 2,300mg-per-day sodium budget. Take a minute to scan the restaurant's nutrition data online, in-store, or from a smart phone.

YOU BUY LEAN COLD CUTS
and pile them high on your sandwich.

Prosciutto
Per ounce: Super-salty at 650mg for two of these paper-thin slices

Honey-Cured Ham
Per ounce: A smidge more sodium than the chicken breast—265mg

THE RESULT

Excess sodium

Oven-Roasted Chicken Breast
Per ounce: Not salt-free at about 243mg. Lower-sodium versions have about 175mg.

THE FIX

The curing of meats was traditionally done to preserve a precious food, and that food, being precious, wasn't served in mile-high deli sandwiches. It's the portion, not the pastrami, that can be unhealthy these days. Still, even in a modest 1- or 2-ounce serving, sodium can add up. **To dodge some of the salt, get slices fresh from the deli for up to 50% sodium savings over pre-sliced.** Opt for reduced-sodium versions when you can. And load your sandwich with lots of veggies.

Soft and Hard Salamis
Per ounce: Starting at 320mg sodium, these options are similar to sausage.

Beef Pastrami
Per ounce: Seasoned brisket or round has less sodium (242mg) than you might think.

Roast Beef
Per ounce: Beef is a salt-savvy choice (166mg). Some reduced-sodium versions have just 40mg.

Smoked Turkey Breast
Per ounce: No sat fat and about 260mg sodium (170mg in lower-sodium versions)

YOU COOK BACON
in a skillet.

THE RESULT

Burned and crinkly bacon

THE FIX

Pan-frying is the standard way to cook bacon, but it has its drawbacks. Only a few strips fit flat in most skillets—any more than that will slope up the sides, cooking unevenly. And bacon strips can shrink more than they need to in a hot pan. (Starting them in a cold pan helps, but you'll still need to flip often.) **Take a cue from chefs—bake your bacon. Heat hits the slices from all sides, cooking them more evenly.** The result: consistently flat strips.

First, line a jelly-roll pan with foil to make cleanup easier. Set a wire rack on the pan so the bacon doesn't sit in fat and so that heat can circulate around the slices. Place bacon slices in a single layer on the rack, and bake at 400° for about 20 minutes (depending on bacon thickness and how crisp you like it). Unless your oven has major hot spots (see page 18 to learn how to find out), you don't have to flip the bacon or turn the pans. You can even put the bacon in while the oven preheats—the gradual temperature increase will render the fat more slowly and won't shrink the meat as much.

YOU SWAP
turkey bacon for pork to save on fat.

THE RESULT

Not always the hefty salt and fat savings you might expect

THE FIX

We're not trying to pick on the poor old turkey here, but bacon is a prime example of why label-reading is important. **Pork bacon comes in smoky, superthick, fatty slabs but also in naturally leaner center-cut slices; the latter can contain as little as 60 calories, 1.5g sat fat, and 260mg sodium per slice.**

Turkey bacon also wanders all over the nutrition map. One ultralean version is a nutritional bargain at 20 calories, 0g sat fat, and 120mg sodium. But others can contain the same amount of sat fat as center-cut pork bacon—and even more sodium. If you like pork, choose a lean, high-flavor cut. If you need less fat, find a lean, lower-sodium turkey product.

Gobble, Gobble

OOPS!

SAUCES, CONDIMENTS & EXTRAS

YOU DON'T WHISK YOUR GRAVY properly.

THE RESULT

Lumps

THE FIX

Lumpy gravy is one of the small culinary tragedies of a meal, often the by-product of a hurried cook. One cause is dumping dry flour, cornstarch, or other thickener directly into the hot stock or broth. Another: adding broth too quickly into a roux—the flour-fat mixture that some gravy recipes start with—which can cause clumping or a gluey layer on the bottom of the pan. Hot spots in a large pan can complicate things as well. **In any starch-based sauce, the thickener needs to be gradually introduced to the hot liquid.** The easiest way involves whisking a flour slurry (a mixture of flour and a small amount of liquid) into the broth mixture, then stirring until the gravy comes together.

If lumps happen, you don't have to take them. Pass gravy through a sieve or strainer, or puree it with an immersion blender or, very carefully, in a regular blender. If the gravy originally contained sautéed mushroom slices, well, the guests needn't know that, and it will still be delicious.

YOU MAKE
FROM-SCRATCH GRAVY
and freeze some for later.

THE RESULT

The gravy separates
when thawed.

THE FIX

Freezing is a great make-ahead strategy, but it's not a panacea. Some foods simply don't freeze well. **Gravies and sauces thickened with cornstarch or flour will separate during the thawing process.** When making the gravy, set aside the amount you plan to freeze before you add the thickeners; then stir them in after thawing.

YOU USE A DARK SKILLET
to brown butter.

THE RESULT

Burned, bitter butter

Browning butter is a sure way to infuse a dish with a great deal of nutty, buttery flavor without using a lot of fat. But the process is a little tricky because once the butter begins to brown, it can race right into burned. Then nutty becomes bitter.

Success depends on visual cues, so use a stainless-steel pan—you can more easily see the butter change color. Use no more than medium heat so that the browning proceeds gradually. First the butter will foam in the pan—the milk solids are separating from the butterfat, and the water is evaporating.

Then the foam subsides and the milk solids begin to brown. Now the butter gives off its characteristic nutty aroma (the French call brown butter *beurre noisette,* or hazelnut butter). Some recipes call for adding lemon juice at this point; the tartness complements the sweet butter, while the juice cools it and slows the browning. Either way, when the butter turns amber brown, take the pan off the heat. If you're not using the butter immediately (say, drizzling it over steamed vegetables), get it out of the hot pan and into a bowl so the residual heat doesn't push the butter from brown to burned.

YOU STORE BUTTER
in the fridge's
butter compartment.

THE RESULT

The butter goes bad.

THE FIX

Air and bright light break down fat molecules and eventually turn butter rancid, which is why it is best stored in a cool, dark place, like the refrigerator. **Since fridge door temperatures vary considerably, skip the butter compartment, and store butter near the back.** Butter tends to absorb odors, so keep it covered and away from strong-smelling foods. In a cold refrigerator, a stick of salted butter in its original wrapping will keep for about 2 months (the salt acts as a preservative); unsalted butter for 1½ months. Butter freezes well for up to 6 months.

YOU SUB
MARGARINE FOR BUTTER
to save on sat fat.

THE RESULT

You may gain trans fat.

THE FIX

Margarine is made by forcing hydrogen through vegetable oils, which makes it solid at room temperature and also produces trans fat, a type of fat that raises "bad" LDL cholesterol and lowers "good" HDL cholesterol. Check ingredients; **many margarines still use these partially hydrogenated oils and can contain up to 2.5g of trans fat per tablespoon.** (The American Heart Association recommends limiting trans fat to less than 1% of your daily calories—about 2g for the average person on a 2,000-calorie-per-day diet.) Other margarines now blend trans-fat-free palm oils with emulsified vegetable oils and are trans fat free.

Butter is made from cream (the fatty top layer of whole milk) that's churned until the fat solids separate. By law, it must contain at least 80% milk fat—artisanal varieties may have more. You can't hide it: Butter contains fat and a good bit of it—7g of sat fat per tablespoon. But in moderate amounts, butter can be part of a healthy diet. There's really no substitute—it produces rich flavors, helps create tender baked goods, and is key for browning.

YOU USE SEASAME AND EXTRA-VIRGIN OLIVE OILS
for all your stir-fries.

THE RESULT

Burned oil

THE FIX

Stir-frying requires high heat to produce the desired effect—fresh, vibrant flavors with a hint of smokiness. But that high heat can wreak havoc on delicate oils like extra-virgin olive oil, walnut oil, and sesame oil that have lower smoke points. **If these oils are used in stir-frying, the result will be diminished—or burned—flavors.** If you love the taste of these oils, add them only at the end or in a marinade. When cooking over high heat, use an all-purpose, neutral-flavored oil such as canola, which has a high smoke point (nearly 470°) and the least sat fat of any oil.

YOU STORE COOKING OILS
in pretty glass containers on the counter.

THE RESULT

Spoiled oils

A clear and present danger

Light, oxygen, and heat are all oil's enemies, causing it to turn rancid. So **instead of clear glass, store oils in tightly sealed, opaque or colored-glass containers in a cool, dry place,** like a cabinet or pantry. If you cook often with a particular oil, store a small amount in an opaque bottle or cruet near the stove, and keep the rest in the cabinet. Some fragile oils, such as toasted nut or seed oils or unfiltered extra-virgin olive oil, have a shorter shelf life than other vegetable oils and require greater precaution. Store these oils in the refrigerator—some will congeal; just be sure to bring them to room temperature before using.

YOU SKIP THE DRESSING
on your salad.

THE RESULT

You may be missing out
on healthy fats and the ability
to absorb the salad's nutrients.

Plain Jane

All dressed up

THE FIX

Salad dressings are all over the nutritional map. Some, such as blue cheese, are hefty in sat fat (1.2g per tablespoon) and others, such as balsamic vinaigrette, provide a good dose of healthy fats (1g of monounsaturated and 1.3g of polyunsaturated, with 0.4g sat fat). When purchasing a bottled dressing, shift your focus away from total fat. The nutrition label's number for total fat includes bad fats *and* good fats, so it is misleading. **Instead, look at the specific types of fat listed under total fat; aim for more mono- and polyunsaturated fats, less saturated, and no trans.** Oil and vinegar–based dressings are generally high in healthy fats. In addition to the good-for-you components of dressings, those fats add rich texture and flavor and also help you absorb the fat-soluble nutrients (vitamins A, D, E, and K) found in salad.

YOU STORE MAPLE SYRUP
in the pantry after it's been opened.

THE RESULT

Moldy syrup

THE FIX

Pure maple syrup is made by boiling water off the sap collected from maple trees, leaving behind an amber-gold liquid and rich flavor, which distinguishes it from maple-*flavored* syrups. **Unopened pure maple syrup can be stored in a cool, dry place indefinitely, but once the seal has been broken, keep syrup in the refrigerator; otherwise you might end up with mold.**

Depending on how badly the mold has penetrated, you may be able to remove it (the rest of the syrup is fine). Skim off the top surface of the syrup where the mold has formed, and discard. Pour the rest of the syrup into a saucepan, and heat until it boils. Cool slightly, and then skim the surface again. Let it cool. Wash the original container in hot, soapy water, and refill with the cooled syrup. Since pure maple syrup won't freeze solid, the freezer is another storage option. It will keep indefinitely in the freezer, but let the syrup come to room temperature or warm it before serving.

YOUR BROWN SUGAR
gets too much air.

THE RESULT

A hard heap

THE FIX

When you find your brown sugar in a brick-like mound, blame improper storage—**exposure to air causes the moisture in the sugar to evaporate.** There are a couple of ways to restore softness. If you need the sugar immediately, place it in a microwave-safe container, cover with a damp (but not dripping) paper towel, and cook at HIGH in 30-second intervals until it's softened. Microwave-softened sugar hardens as it cools, so only heat the amount you need. A longer method with more lasting results: Add an apple slice to the container, seal, and wait a day or so. The sugar will absorb the moisture from the apple. In the future, make sure you store brown sugar in an airtight container in a cool, dry place (but not in the refrigerator).

YOU SKIP PEANUT BUTTER
because it's high in calories and fat.

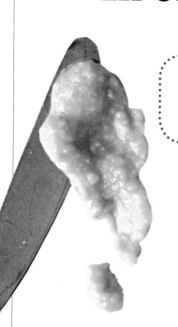

THE RESULT

You miss out on healthy fats and filling protein.

THE FIX

At 95 calories per tablespoon, peanut butter (and other nut butters) may be caloric, but those calories come with nutrients that are not worth sacrificing to the scale. **Nut butters are packed with satiating protein and fiber (4g and 1g per tablespoon, respectively) to help keep your stomach from rumbling between meals and are a great source of heart-healthy fats.** Pick a natural nut butter that includes only nuts (and occasionally sugar and salt) in the ingredient list. Before spreading it on your sandwich, give it a good stir to incorporate the oils that may have separated. (Store it in the fridge to keep the oils from separating again.) Some commercial peanut butter and nut butter varieties contain trans fat that should be avoided since it raises levels of bad cholesterol while decreasing good cholesterol. The way to tell if trans fat is lurking: The ingredient list will include partially hydrogenated oils. *Fully* hydrogenated oils do not contain trans fat.

YOU BUY PEANUT BUTTER FORTIFIED WITH OMEGA-3S
to get your share of good fats.

THE RESULT

You may not be getting as many omega-3s as you think.

THE FIX

Fortification of foods is sometimes good but can also be marketed a bit... enthusiastically. **You'd have to eat 1 cup of peanut butter—a whopping 1,520 calories—to equal the amount of omega-3s in a 4-ounce serving of salmon** that has about 200 calories. Enjoy the PB, but favor the fish.

YOU CHECK EMAIL
while you're toasting nuts.

THE FIX

Toasting intensifies the flavor of nuts, allowing us to use less in our recipes (and thus lower calories). But the nut is a mighty delicate thing—in an oven it can go from perfectly toasty to charred in seconds. It happens to even the most experienced cooks. Our preferred method: Arrange nuts in a single layer on a heavy baking sheet, and bake at 350° for as little as 2 minutes for pine nuts to 5 or more minutes for dense nuts such as almonds. Shake the pan or stir frequently so the nuts toast evenly—they tend to brown on the bottom more quickly. **They're done when they've darkened slightly (or turned golden brown for pale nuts such as pine nuts or slivered almonds) and smell fragrant and toasty.** Do not start another project or walk away while they're in the oven. One final word: If you burn the nuts, toss and start over—you don't want that acrid quality in your food. Oh, and another final word: We don't recommend toasting in a pan on the stovetop since it's almost impossible not to burn them that way.

Toasty!

YOU SPOON WHOLE FLAXSEEDS on your cereal.

THE RESULT

The omega-3s are tourists—they don't hang around.

THE FIX

Flaxseeds are trendy, marketed as something of a superfood. They are an excellent way to add fiber and omega-3 fatty acids to baked goods, oatmeal, and cereal. And they're a good alternative to fish and fish oils for vegetarians and vegans. But whole seeds tend to, um, pass right through...you. **To unlock the goodness, grind the seeds.**

YOU SPRINKLE WHEAT GERM
on yogurt or muffins for crunchy, whole-grain goodness.

THE FIX

A whole grain is a seed with three parts: bran, endosperm, and germ. **Wheat germ is only one component of a whole grain.** Most of the fiber is in the bran, and the protein is in the endosperm. Wheat germ delivers a concentrated wallop of folate and vitamin E but doesn't count as a whole grain. So enjoy it, but not at the expense of other whole-grain choices.

THE RESULT

A good nutrient boost, but not quite a whole grain

YOU THINK COARSE SEA SALTS AND KOSHER SALT
contain more sodium so you stick with table salt.

THE RESULT

You get 20% more sodium.

Size does matter.

THE FIX

Kosher and table salts are chemically the same. But the larger grain size of kosher salt actually works to your advantage. **Tiny grains of table salt tend to pack down in the spoon, leaving less air. Coarse flakes and crystals pile up like little, rough rocks, with more air between the pieces.** That adds up to 20% sodium savings measure for measure. Have fun exploring the sea and rock salts on the market. Stronger flavor means you can use less, too.

YOUR SODIUM-REDUCTION STRATEGY IS TO ADD less table salt to your meals.

It's not your fault.

THE RESULT

Less savings than you think

THE FIX

Don't blame the salt shaker. **The real culprits to watch out for are processed and restaurant foods, which deliver 77% of the sodium in the average American diet—only 10% to 11% is added at the table.** The rest is added by cooks during meal prep or occurs naturally in foods. Odds are more than 50-50 that you're on the list of people who need to watch their salt. The government's Dietary Guidelines recommend no more than 2,300mg of sodium per day for adults, but there's a *huge* asterisk: The level for African-Americans, people with hypertension, and anyone over the age of 51 is 1,500mg. That's basically *half*. Yet the average American's consumption is 3,400mg.

OOPS!

BEVERAGES, SNACKS & DESSERTS

YOU BOLSTER YOUR IMMUNE
system with extra vitamin C.

THE RESULT

You still find yourself with the sniffles.

THE FIX

Keep your vitamin C levels under control: 75mg per day is recommended for women, and 90mg for men. **Extra vitamin C hasn't been proven to prevent colds.** (Exceeding 2,000mg per day can cause nausea and other gastrointestinal problems.) What has been proven to work? Washing your hands.

YOU GUZZLE PULPY OJ
to up your fiber intake.

THE RESULT

Lots of vitamin C but no fiber

Not much fiber found here.

THE FIX

Even though the pulpy stuff seems like it would contain fiber, it doesn't. **Most of the fiber in an orange actually comes from pectin in the white inner portion of the peel that surrounds the segments.** This fuzzy layer, called the albedo, is removed in the juicing process, along with the fiber (2.5g per medium orange). With or without the pulp, 4 ounces of fresh orange juice may not offer any fiber, but it does supply 83% of your daily vitamin C—about the same as the whole fruit.

YOU AVOID JUICE
from concentrate.

THE RESULT

You miss out on a good
form of juice.

Juice made from concentrate is the same as the original juice. The only thing missing is most of the water. Extracting water reduces juice volume and weight, making it easier to ship. When water is added back to the concentrate, the product is labeled "reconstituted" or "made from concentrate" and generally has the same nutrition profile as the original juice. The exception is if sugar is added when the juice is reconstituted. Check the ingredient list to be sure.

I'm just as good as juice.

YOU DRINK GREEN TEA
for the antioxidants.

THE RESULT

Not as much proven benefit
as you think

THE FIX

Despite the marketing hype, the jury's still out on the health benefits of drinking green tea. One of the tea's compounds, EGCG (or epigallocatechin gallate), has been widely touted by the beverage industry and by nutrition research as a powerful antioxidant, but most of these studies have been done in a lab, not on humans. More research is under way, but for now, only preliminary findings have linked green tea to delaying or preventing the growth of certain cancers, slowing weight gain, and lowering blood pressure. Fewer results are available for decaffeinated green teas, but the beverage's likely benefits come from the antioxidants, not the caffeine. Even though the benefits aren't proven, that's no reason not to drink up. Green tea does contain antioxidants important for good health. And because of green tea's minimal processing, these healthful compounds are more concentrated.

YOU SQUEEZE TEA BAGS
to extract every last bit of flavor.

THE RESULT

Bitter tea

THE FIX

Putting the squeeze on a tea bag may make it less messy to dispose of, but that little bit of trapped tea can bring bitterness to your cup. Tea contains tannins, plant polyphenols that have a bitter, astringent taste. **Squeezing the bag after steeping releases a bit of well-steeped liquid that's higher in these tannins.** Another possible result: The tea bag could break, adding more than you bargained for to your cup.

YOU USE PREVIOUSLY BOILED
water to make tea.

THE RESULT

Flat-tasting tea

THE FIX

Water that's been previously boiled—like the water in your teakettle—makes a dull-flavored tea. Here's why: As water boils, oxygen is driven out; the longer it boils, the less oxygen remains. The aromatic compounds in tea react with the oxygen in the water to produce flavor. Without oxygen, those compounds can't bind to the water molecules, leaving you with tea that lacks that fresh, crisp taste. For better-tasting tea, use fresh water every time.

YOU PLACE HOT TEA
in the fridge to cool.

THE RESULT

Cloudy iced tea

THE FIX

One of the causes of cloudy tea is the antioxidant theaflavin. **If tea is cooled too quickly, the theaflavin reacts with the caffeine, forming particles that make tea cloudy.** However, when tea is kept at higher temperatures or cooled slowly, the theaflavin will remain suspended. To avoid cloudiness, let tea cool to room temperature, and then chill. Or cold-brew tea: Fill a pitcher with cold water, add tea bags, and let it steep for at least six hours. If tea is already cloudy, you can fix it by adding a little boiling water. The cloudiness doesn't affect flavor, so if the appearance doesn't bother you, then don't worry about fixing it.

YOU OFTEN UPGRADE YOUR
coffee to a flavored latte.

THE RESULT

Your latte isn't as skinny
as you think.

WHIPPED CREAM
60 calories & 4g sat fat

1 SUGAR PACKET
11 calories & 3g carbs

MADE WITH WHOLE MILK
80 calories & 5g sat fat

MADE WITH 2% MILK
50 calories & 3.5g sat fat

1 PUMP OF SYRUP
20 calories & 5g carbs

THE FIX

Seemingly small upgrades to your morning coffee can amp up the calorie load more than you may think. A 12-ounce serving of brewed coffee clocks in at less than 5 calories; the addition of a tablespoon of full-fat half-and-half and one sugar packet brings the total calories to less than 35. But if you upgrade to a skinny latte, the total goes to 100. Make it a full-fat latte, and you increase it to 180. Add on whipped cream, and it's now at 240. A pump of syrup adds 20 more calories. When it comes to building your latte, do the math and know how many calories you're willing to devote to your morning cup of joe.

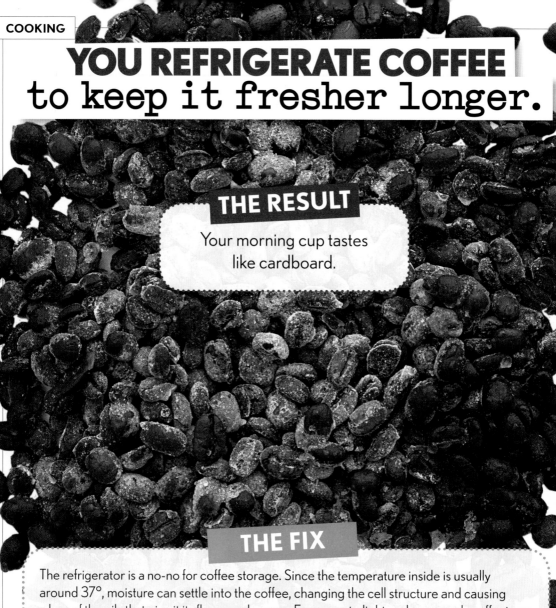

YOU REFRIGERATE COFFEE
to keep it fresher longer.

THE RESULT

Your morning cup tastes like cardboard.

THE FIX

The refrigerator is a no-no for coffee storage. Since the temperature inside is usually around 37°, moisture can settle into the coffee, changing the cell structure and causing a loss of the oils that give it its flavor and aroma. Exposure to light and oxygen also affect flavor. **The best way to store coffee is at room temperature in an opaque, air-tight container in a cool, dark place like a pantry or cabinet.** (If you don't have a coffee canister, store the bag of coffee in a zip-top plastic bag.) Room-temp storage is ideal for coffee that will be consumed in one to two weeks. The freezer is a good option for long-term storage (up to one month) but not for your everyday coffee because the fluctuating temperatures can create moisture in the container. It's best to thaw coffee only once, right before you plan to use it.

YOU GRIND COFFEE BEANS
for the week all at once.

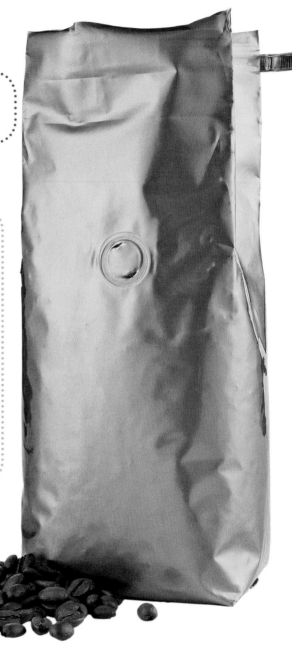

THE RESULT

Less flavorful coffee

THE FIX

Store beans in an airtight canister away from light, and then grind just before brewing. **Once ground, more of the bean's surface area is exposed to air, causing the oils (and the flavor) to evaporate faster.** Ground coffee lasts just a day or two at room temperature; whole beans, up to two weeks. Using higher-quality beans and better machines makes for richer flavor, but good coffeehouses use more coffee when brewing, too: 2 tablespoons of coffee per 6 ounces of water.

YOU SKIP
CAFFEINATED BEVERAGES
when you need hydration.

THE RESULT

You miss out on some
tasty drink options.

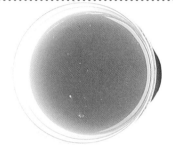

THE FIX

Caffeinated beverages can indeed hydrate you as well as water—provided you don't drink them in excess. Researchers used to believe that any caffeinated beverage, like soda or coffee, had a diuretic effect, meaning you'd urinate more after drinking it, increasing your risk of dehydration. But recent research has shown this to be true only if you drink large amounts—more than 500 to 600mg per day, the equivalent of 11 diet sodas or more than 5 cups of home-brewed coffee.

YOU DOWN A SPORTS DRINK
after your 30–minute
workout.

THE RESULT

More liquid calories
than you need

THE FIX

Sports drinks contain carbohydrates and electrolytes, such as sodium, potassium, and chloride, and are designed to rehydrate and keep energy levels high. Electrolytes assist in cellular function and regulate fluid balance—life-saving in cases of severe fluid loss. They're also lost through sweat during exercise. However, **unless you're active at a high intensity for more than 60 minutes per workout or are exercising in very hot conditions, you don't need sports drinks.** Water and a balanced diet will keep you hydrated and supply all the electrolytes you need.

If you're concerned about calories—and that's one reason you're at the gym in the first place—read the labels. To provide bona fide energy, a drink must contain calories, and that usually means sugar. Some beverages have two to three servings per bottle. If you drink the whole bottle, that can easily translate to more than 200 calories, which could be more than you burned during your workout.

YOU CHOOSE LIGHTER-COLORED BEER OVER DARK
to save on calories.

THE RESULT

Not much of the calorie
savings you covet

THE FIX

Color doesn't tell the whole tale. Guinness Stout looks dark and heavy but has about the same calories as Bud Light. What can compound the confusion is a lack of consistent labeling. A Bud Light label lists calories but not alcohol (4.2% compared to a regular Bud's 5%), while a 12-ounce bottle of specialty ale may state its alcohol content (a walloping 8%) but not reveal calories. Confused? So were we. If the label doesn't list calories, look to the alcohol percentages to guide you instead. ***As a general rule*, more alcohol means more calories.** To keep your number in check (and keep things simple), heed the Dietary Guidelines for Americans, which recommend the alcohol equivalent of up to one beer a day for women (two for men), defined as 12 ounces of regular beer with 5% alcohol by volume (ABV).

YOU ASSUME THE ONLY HEART-FRIENDLY ALCOHOL
is red wine.

Demoted

THE RESULT

You miss out on beer, white wine, and liquors, which all have benefits.

THE FIX

The so-called French Paradox elevated red wine to health-food status when researchers thought it was the antioxidants in the drink that protected the foie gras– and cheese-loving French from heart disease. More recent research, however, has shown that antioxidants aren't the answer after all. Alcohol—the ethanol itself—raises levels of protective high-density lipoproteins (HDL, or good cholesterol), which help protect against plaque buildup in the arteries and reduce clotting factors that contribute to stroke and heart attack. **Any kind of beverage that contains alcohol, when consumed in moderation (and that means one to two drinks per day), helps reduce heart disease risk.**

YOU SKIP THE SNACKS
to drop pounds.

A skimpy snack

THE RESULT

Less weight-loss success, more hunger and fatigue

A little more substantial

THE FIX

It's a long stretch from a noontime lunch to a 7 p.m. dinner. Snacking helps manage hunger by keeping your metabolic engine running at a more constant pace, which means you won't attack dinner like a ravenous wolf, so don't skip or skimp. **Any healthy-eating plan should allow for one or two snacks a day— something nutritious and satisfying.** What to snack on: calcium-rich, low-fat dairy foods; full-of-fiber nuts; or naturally sweet, low-calorie fruit.

YOU GO OVERBOARD
on healthy snacks.

THE RESULT

Healthy choice made,
unhealthy quantity consumed

THE FIX

Here's the scenario: Microwave kettle corn that's 94% fat free, to take just one example, saves you 6g of sat fat over the full-fat variety. But a typical, not-very-big bag contains two servings of about 3 cups each. Said handy bag often joins the eater on the couch for a movie, and soon it's empty. It's just human nature to eat what a container contains. **Cornell University portion guru Brian Wansink, PhD, found that people ate as much as 31% more when they used a large bowl.** And he found that people who snacked while watching TV tended to eat 28% more. When snacking, choose that healthier snack *and* eat it in measured amounts.

YOU ALWAYS OPT FOR PRETZELS
as your healthy snack.

THE RESULT

A middle-of-the-road
choice, nutritionally

THE FIX

Compared to a piece of fruit and handful of nuts or cheese and whole-grain crackers, pretzels aren't the healthiest option. But **compared to a trans-fat-filled, high-calorie snack cake with "crème" filling and frosting, pretzels are nutritional manna, especially if you're at a vending machine,** where pretzels may be the lesser of many evils. The biggest rub is that a 1-ounce serving of pretzels has 110 calories and 450mg sodium—about one-fifth of your daily sodium allotment. Choose low-salt or unsalted multigrain and whole-grain versions for the biggest nutritional boost.

WHEN MAKING POPCORN,
you eyeball the oil.

Oil slick

THE RESULT

Popcorn that has an oily film

Excess oil can leave you with a pile of greasy popcorn—not the tasty snack you'd envisioned. To get perfect popcorn every time, you need a deep 8-quart pot or Dutch oven that has a large surface area on the bottom and a tightly fitting lid. Add just enough oil to cover the bottom of the pan—about 1 to 2 teaspoons per ¼ cup popcorn kernels. **Add the popcorn kernels and stir them to make sure all sides are coated with oil—they should be in a single layer, not piled on top of each other.** Cover with the lid, and cook over medium heat, shaking the pan to ensure the heat reaches all sides of the kernels. Once they start to pop, shake the pan again

so the kernels on the bottom don't burn. It'll take just a few minutes for the popping to stop. Remove from heat, toss with a bit of kosher salt or Parmesan cheese, if you like, and enjoy.

Popcorn cooked this way has 0.2g saturated fat in 3½ cups, and you enjoy a whole-grain serving with 4 grams of fiber. To compare, 94% fat-free microwave popcorns is nearly as good. Full-fat microwave popcorn contains 4.5g of saturated and trans fats combined. At the extreme: Movie theaters drench a 7-cup "small" serving with 29 grams of saturated fat in the form of "butter topping," almost as much as a behemoth fast-food burger boasts.

Popped right

YOU ALWAYS SPLURGE
on chips and dip at Mexican restaurants.

THE RESULT

You may be getting *way* more calories than you think.

THE FIX

Crunchy, corny, oily, salty—i.e., totally irresistible—tortilla chips usually start dinner at the local cantina. Halfway into a basket, you're in for more than 300 calories and, at 200mg, the sodium's starting to add up before you've touched the guac or downed a margarita. **We measured chip baskets and found that a quarter-basket represents about a 1-ounce serving—1¼ ounces to be precise. It's a sensible portion containing 169 calories.** So visualize a quarter-basket when you sit down, and savor each crunch. Pay attention to the dips as well: A 2-tablespoon serving of salsa has 10 calories, guac comes in at 50 calories, and queso clocks in at 70.

YOU SKIP A PREWORKOUT SNACK
to save on calories.

Banana + PB
= 200 calories

THE RESULT

Fewer calories in can mean fewer calories burned.

THE FIX

Think of a preworkout snack as fueling, not filling, says fitness expert Myatt Murphy, CSCS. **Although you exercise to burn calories, to exercise effectively and burn even more, you need a few calories in the tank.** A 100- to 200-calorie snack is just enough to give you energy for exercise. Too much food and your stomach will also be working out—trying to digest the food.

The best time to eat a snack is 30 minutes before exercising. If you're an early bird, a snack is essential since you're running on empty. If you exercise mid-afternoon, you might need less. The best snack provides a mix of carbs and protein—a banana or a slice of whole-grain bread and peanut butter or a handful of nuts.

YOU FOLLOW UP
A 300-CALORIE WORKOUT
with a 300-calorie treat.

It'll take an hour to walk this off.

THE RESULT

More calories in than out

THE FIX

Cardio-equipment calorie counters are notorious for overestimating calorie burn. The American Council on Exercise found that some machines can be off by 25%. Machines that require you to punch in your weight, height, age, and gender give you a better estimate, but it's still an estimate, so don't assume you can eat a treat with equivalent calories as a "freebie." If you're counting calories, invest in a heart-rate monitor, the kind that straps around your chest, to get an accurate measurement.

YOU ASSUME ADDED SUGAR
is always bad for you.

THE RESULT

Less-tasty food

Just enough

THE FIX

Sugar is essential in the kitchen. Consider all it does for baking—creates a tender cake crumb and ensures crisp cookies, for example. Then there's its role in creating airy meringue or soft-textured ice cream. Keep in mind that other sweeteners like "natural" honey are basically refined sugar anyway, and they're all metabolized by your body the same way. Sugar also balances flavors in healthy foods that might not taste so great on their own. A wee bit of sugar to balance a savory tomato sauce is a good thing, as is a teaspoon of honey on a tart grapefruit half or in plain yogurt. **Don't go overboard, of course.** Most health experts suggest that added sugar supply no more than 10% of your total calories—about 200 in a 2,000-calorie diet.

YOU ALWAYS CHOOSE
sorbet over ice cream.

I'm low-fat.

THE RESULT

You miss out on ice cream's nutritious qualities.

I've got protein *and* calcium.

THE FIX

The beauty of sorbet lies in its simplicity: It's basically just frozen, sweetened fruit juice. However, while sorbet is "light" in the fat department, keep in mind that it's not like eating fruit. It does contain calories, mostly from sugar—many sorbets contain three times more calories (thanks to added sugar) and fewer vitamins (thanks to the extra water) than 1 cup of the actual fruit. **Compared to ice cream, sorbet saves on calories and saturated fat, but you'll also see less protein and calcium**—½ cup of ice cream contains 2 to 4g of protein and 80 to 130mg calcium. Plus, the amount of sugar in ice creams and sorbets is about the same.

YOU GET YOUR FRUIT
servings from products
"made with real fruit."

Missing:
the fruit

THE RESULT

Not always much fruit

THE FIX

Some seemingly fruity foods may contain as little as 2% real fruit. Or the fruit may be juice concentrate, a form of sugar. Bottom line: Check the ingredients to see how far down the "real" fruit falls on the list.

OOPS!

BAKING

YOU EYEBALL
ingredients.

THE RESULT

Dry, tough cakes; rubbery brownies; and a host of other textural mishaps

A cup of all-purpose flour should weigh 4.5 ounces, while a cup of whole-wheat flour weighs slightly more, at 4.75 ounces per cup.

THE FIX

In lighter baking, you're using less butter and oil—ingredients that can hide a host of measurement sins. Adding as little as 2 extra tablespoons of flour to a cake recipe can leave you with a dry, tough texture. And adding extra is easy: One cook's cup of flour may be another's 1¼ cups. The discrepancy comes in how each cook scoops out the flour. Some people scoop flour from the canister and pack it down into the cup or tap it on the counter and then add more. Both practices yield too much flour.

Weighing is the most accurate way to measure, but if you don't have a kitchen scale, the best method is to lightly spoon the flour into a dry measuring cup—meaning, don't pack it in there—and then level with the flat side of a knife. If you are measuring by weight, it's not important how you get the flour out of the canister.

YOU STORE
all your flours in the pantry.

THE RESULT

You find a funky smell emanating from the flour.

THE FIX

That smell is rancid flour. Light and heat speed up the decay of flour, and it's faster yet in whole-grain varieties. The reason: **The higher fat content (from the oil in the grain) makes these flours more susceptible to spoilage.** Always store them in airtight containers in the refrigerator or freezer, and bring them back to room temperature before using them. Refined flours that have been stripped of the bran and germ (all-purpose, cake, pastry, and bread) are more stable and can be stored in a cool, dry place (no warmer than 75°).

YOU MICROWAVE
butter to soften it.

THE RESULT

Cookies spread too much
and cakes are too dense.

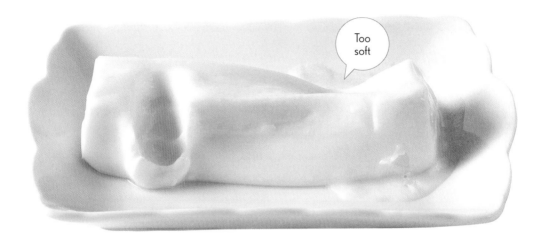

Too
soft

THE FIX

We've all done it—forgotten to soften the butter and zapped it in the microwave to do the job quickly. But this seemingly time-saving task can backfire when the butter softens too much (or worse, melts). It really is better to let it stand at room temperature for 30 to 45 minutes to get the right consistency. You can speed the process significantly by cutting the butter into tablespoon-sized portions before letting it stand. (But don't let it get too warm; see page 248.)

Properly softened butter should yield slightly to gentle pressure, but you don't want to be able to sink your finger way down into it. Too-soft butter means that cookie dough will be more like batter, and it will spread too much and lose shape as it bakes. It also won't cream properly with sugar, and creaming is essential to creating tender cakes and cookies with a delicate crumb.

YOU BOIL
low-fat milk products.

Those grainy bits are curdled milk.

THE RESULT

The milk curdles or "breaks," yielding grainy mac and cheese, ice cream, or pudding.

THE FIX

Even though you can boil cream just fine, the same isn't true for other milk products, which will curdle. A distracted cook can quickly end up with a grainy, broken mess. **The solution is to heat lower-fat dairy products to no more than 180°.** Use a clip-on thermometer, hover over the pan, and cook over medium-low or low heat to prevent curdling. If the milk curdles, toss and start again: Ice cream or pudding made with curdled milk won't ever be smooth or velvety. One alternative: Stabilize milk with starch, such as cornstarch or flour, if you want to bring it to a boil; the starch will prevent curdling, and it'll thicken the milk, too.

YOU DOUBLE THE RECIPE
for baked goods.

THE RESULT

They don't turn out quite right.

THE FIX

It's not that uncommon to double a recipe for a dinner party or halve it when you're only serving two. It's basically just a matter of math and measurements, right? Yes and no. It's no big deal in many dishes, but it's not universally true, particularly in baking. **Doubling or halving a recipe changes the calculated chemistry of the ingredients and affects the rate at which they cook.** For example, doubling a quick bread recipe and then creating a larger, wider loaf increases the surface area that's exposed to the heat, changing the rate at which it cooks. The best advice when it comes to scaling recipes in baking is not to do it. If you must increase the quantity, make the same recipe in multiple batches.

YOU MAKE SUBSTITUTIONS
to lighten your favorite full-fat recipes.

THE RESULT

You wreck the underlying chemistry of the dish.

Gummy and dense

Good

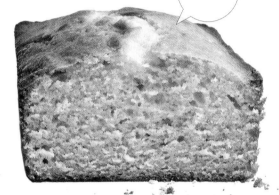

THE FIX

Substitutions are a particular temptation and challenge with healthy cooking. **When it comes to light baking in particular, smart substitutions are as much a science as an art, and require a lot of trial and error.** We learn a lot from reader disappointments. Calls about cakes turning out too dense or too gummy may lead us to find that the reader used *all* applesauce instead of a mix of applesauce and oil or butter, subbed whole-wheat flour for all-purpose where that just wouldn't do, or went with sugar substitute in place of sugar. Too much applesauce makes baked goods gummy, too much whole-wheat flour can make them dense, and sugar substitutes don't react the same way as sugar. All three mistakes in one cupcake recipe add up to clay, not cake. The best practice: Follow the recipe, period. And if you want to experiment (and please do!), regard it as that and expect a few failures along the way.

YOU MIX DOUGH VIGOROUSLY
to incorporate the ingredients.

THE RESULT

Tough cookies, scones, piecrusts, and biscuits

Gluten overload

THE FIX

Recipes with lots of butter are more likely to stay moist and tender because of the fat, even if the dough is overmixed and overkneaded, but in light baking, you absolutely must use a light hand. **Vigorous mixing encourages gluten development, which creates a chewy or tough texture—great in a baguette but not in a biscuit.** That's why many of our biscuit and scone recipes instruct the cook to knead the dough gently or pat it out instead of rolling, and our cookie and piecrust recipes say to mix just until the flour is incorporated. To be safe, stop machine-mixing early and finish the last bit by hand. It really does make a difference.

YOU WHIP COLD
egg whites.

THE RESULT

Meringue doesn't form, cake layers fall flat, soufflés have no lift.

Whipped

Warped

THE FIX

Properly beaten egg whites are voluminous, creamy, and glossy, but they require care. First, separate whites from yolks carefully; a speck of yolk can prevent the whites from whipping up fully. (See our preferred egg separation method on page 117.) **After separating, let the whites stand for a few minutes. When they're at room temperature they whip up better than when cold.** Whip with clean, dry beaters at high speed just until stiff peaks form—that is, until the peak created when you lift the beater out of the bowl stands upright. If you overbeat, the whites will turn grainy or dry, or they may separate. When the whites are perfectly beaten, gently fold them into the cake batter or soufflé base. Otherwise, you'll deflate them.

YOUR WAFFLE BATTER
is too thick.

THE RESULT

Raw in the middle

Oozing

Crisp!

THE FIX

Compared to muffins, waffles have a higher liquid-to-dry ingredient ratio. When this ratio gets out of whack and the dry ingredients outweigh the liquid, the result is a doughy or undercooked center. **To make sure your waffles get golden-brown (or even almost crispy, depending on how you like them), shoot for a batter that is still slightly thick but pourable and that spreads easily on the waffle iron.** If after following the recipe, your batter still seems too thick, add additional milk by tablespoons until the batter reaches the desired consistency. Keep the cooked waffles warm by putting them on a metal baking pan or oven-safe platter in an oven preheated to 200°.

YOUR FLAPJACKS
flame out.

THE RESULT

Pale or burned pancakes

The dog's breakfast

Good as gold!

THE FIX

Too often, pancakes cook up with a few splotchy specimens at the beginning and a few more duds at the end that emerge scorched on the outside but underdone within. **This is not a heat problem or a batter problem; it's a pan-prepping problem.**

The solution: Don't pour oil directly into the pan—it will pool in some areas and leave other parts dry. Instead, use our method that requires a scant amount of oil to create a smooth, even cooking surface so pancakes cook evenly from start to finish. (If you're using a pristine pan, you may not need oil at all.)

Heat a skillet (any variety) over medium heat; then grasp a wadded paper towel with tongs and douse it with 1 tablespoon canola oil. Brush the pan with the soaked towel. Cooking spray also works, but don't use it on nonstick pans; it leaves a sticky residue.

Add the batter, flipping only when bubbles form on the surface of each pancake (about 2 to 3 minutes). Resist the urge to peek, which breaks the seal between the pan and the batter; that seal is what ensures even cooking. Swab the pan with the oiled paper towel between batches to keep it properly greased.

YOU TAKE BREADS OUT EARLY
rather than risk overbaking.

THE RESULT

They turn out pallid and gummy.

Pale = undercooked

Perfectly browned

THE FIX

Overcooked baked goods disappoint, but we've found that less experienced bakers are more likely to undercook them—and that's a travesty. Many culinary pleasures come from having the confidence to fully cook food: Think about the joy of breaking into a crusty baguette, relishing the sugar crust that tops pound cake, and savoring the crunch of crisped, warm corn bread. **The key is to really look at the food. Even if the wooden pick comes out clean, if the food is pale, it's not finished. Let it go another couple of minutes until it has an even golden-brownness.** It's better to err on the side of slightly overcooking than ending up with gummy, wet, unappealing food. Once you've done this a few times and know exactly what you're looking for, it'll become second nature.

YOUR BLUEBERRIES
take a dive.

THE RESULT

Bottom-heavy muffins

Grounded

Unsinkable

THE FIX

Nothing brightens a bite of a summertime muffin quite like fresh blueberries, unless you discover they've sunk to the bottom, where they've congregated into a mush pile. The cause of sinkage is, in a sense, the season itself: In the heart of summer, fat, ripe berries may be more dense than the batter, causing them to drop. **A dash of flour will help blueberries defy gravity simply because the flour makes them stick to the batter and stay put.** Just toss blueberries with a tablespoon of flour before folding them into the batter. But use flour from the recipe—don't add in extra—to maintain the right ratio of ingredients.

YOU COOL MUFFINS
and cupcakes completely in the pan.

THE RESULT

Soggy baked goods

Wet bottom

THE FIX

When left in the pan too long, the steam inside muffins or cupcakes can't escape and they sit in the pan and sweat, which leaves you with a wet base. Instead, let them cool 5 minutes in the pan, and then transfer them to a wire rack. Cooling on a wire rack allows air to circulate around them, letting the steam escape and leaving you with muffins and cupcakes that have a delicious crumb.

Good crumb

YOU USE YELLOW BANANAS
to make banana bread.

THE RESULT

Chunks of banana, rather
than banana-y goodness
throughout

Chunky

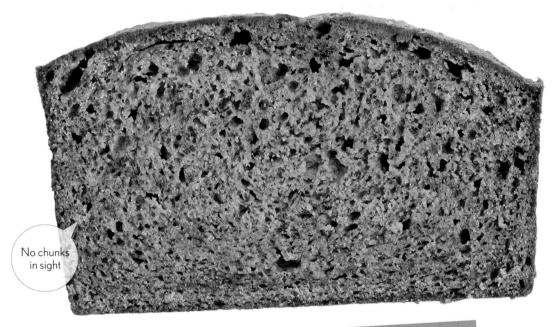

No chunks in sight

THE FIX

Over-the-hill bananas, with their black-speckled (or totally black) peels and squishy flesh, may not be the best for eating out of hand, but they're ideal when making banana bread. **The soft flesh and broken-down starch from the ripened bananas mash easily and mix into the batter smoothly, distributing banana flavor and sweetness throughout.** Unripe bananas lack the sweetness that develops as the bananas ripen, and the flesh will stay in chunks, leaving you with less overall flavor. To keep bananas from getting too ripe, stick them in the refrigerator or freezer. The peel will turn black, but the pulp won't discolor.

YOU TWIST THE BISCUIT CUTTER
to get a sharp, clean cut.

THE RESULT

Biscuits lacking volume
and flakiness

Fab flakiness

THE FIX

Biscuit cutters (and even drinking glasses) are ideal for creating perfect rounds of biscuit dough. **But resist the urge to twist.** That simple movement presses the edges of the dough together, creating tiny seals that prohibit the dough from rising to its maximum flaky peak. Instead, gently press the cutter straight down. The sides of the dough will have slightly ragged edges that allow for those luscious layers to form as the dough rises. See page 232 for more biscuit-making tips.

YOU CHUCK CHOCOLATE AFTER
the white coating appears.

THE RESULT

Perfectly good chocolate ends up in the trash.

Bothersome bloom

THE FIX

Some foods that change color are destined for the trash—moldy bread, brown lettuce. However, in chocolate's case, discoloration isn't always a bad thing. When chocolate is opened and left at a warmer temperature, some of the fat on the surface melts and recrystallizes, leaving behind a white substance (referred to as bloom). **Unless the chocolate is far beyond its expiration date, it's fine to use in baking. The bloom will disappear as soon as the chocolate is melted.** Or simply wipe it off with a damp paper towel. To prevent chocolate from developing bloom or losing flavor, keep it in an airtight container in a cool area or in the refrigerator, and keep an eye on the "use by" date.

YOU MELT CHOCOLATE OVER
high heat to save time.

THE RESULT

The chocolate becomes grainy, separated, or scorched.

Smooth and melty

Grainy and gross

THE FIX

It's very easy to ruin chocolate, and there's no road back. **The best way to melt chocolate is to go slowly, heat gently, remove it from the heat before it's fully melted, and stir until smooth.** If using the microwave, proceed with caution, stopping every 20 to 30 seconds to stir. If using a double boiler, make sure the water is simmering, not boiling.

YOU SKIMP ON THE FAT
when making cookies.

THE RESULT

Cakey texture

THE FIX

The texture of cookies—cakey, crispy, chewy—depends partially on the fat and the number of eggs used in the dough. **Fat plays a major role in how much a cookie spreads.** In general, more fat yields flat, crispy cookies as the butter melts, causing the dough to spread, while less fat means less spreading and puffier, cakelike cookies. Many cookie recipes use a combination of oil and butter, which creates a soft and tender cookie without excess spreading because the oil disperses throughout the dough. The fat and protein in egg yolks bind the dough, give it richness, and create a crisp cookie, while egg whites have a drying effect that makes cookies cakey.

Another cause of cakey cookies: Too much flour. Even an extra tablespoon or two can be too much for a cookie dough, so be sure you're measuring accurately. (See page 226.)

YOU EYEBALL COOKIE
dough portions.

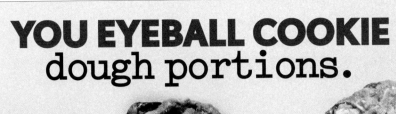

Doughy and soft

THE RESULT

Uneven results

THE FIX

Besides producing cookies that aren't uniform, **unevenly portioned dough bakes at different rates, potentially leaving you with some cookies that are overdone while others are still soft and doughy.** A small ice-cream scoop is a helpful tool if you bake cookies often. It allows you to portion the dough quickly and evenly.

Overcooked

YOU USE WARM OR ROOM-TEMPERATURE BUTTER
in cookie dough.

THE RESULT

Your cookies gain unwanted holiday width.

Never leaving the kitchen

Fit to share

THE FIX

Baking holiday cookies can go from a labor of love to an exercise in frustration when your gingerbread men come out more bloated than a Macy's parade float. The problem is too much heat—not at the baking stage but at the mixing stage: The butter is too warm.

Keep butter cool, right until baking. Butter starts to melt at 68°, and once that happens, its water-fat emulsion breaks, and there's no getting it back. Cold, emulsified butter helps give baked goods structure by taking in air when mixed with sugar. For cookies, you want butter well below room temperature; between 50° and 65° is optimal. Cut the butter into chunks, and let it stand at room temperature to soften—nix the microwave idea entirely. (See page 228 for more information on oversoftening.) If the butter is still cool to the touch but spreadable, you can start creaming. Butter and sugar need to be mixed (or "creamed") for only about 30 seconds—much longer and the butter warms up. Chill the dough for 20 to 30 minutes before baking.

YOU USE A STANDARD STAINLESS-STEEL KNIFE
to cut brownies.

THE RESULT

Mangled edges

Damaged goods

THE FIX

That gooey, sticky quality that endears brownies to us is also the reason they often end up in sloppy squares when they're cut. The culprit is likely the metal knife you're using, particularly if you're cutting still-warm brownies, which don't hold together as well as cooled ones. **The secret weapon: a plastic knife or thin silicone spatula.** Both lack sharp edges for the brownie bits to cling to, so they cut more smoothly through without picking up crumbs, and they work even if you're cutting brownies that haven't completely cooled. Plus, plastic and silicone won't damage pans like metal knives will.

YOU USE A DARK PAN
for baking.

THE RESULT

A too-brown cake

Unfortunate

Golden!

THE FIX

A darker pan absorbs and retains more heat, causing the exterior of the cake to brown (or burn) before the inside is done. But you don't have to ditch your dark pans. **The trick to evening the playing field is adjusting the oven temperature.** If you bake in either dark metal pans or glass dishes, reduce the oven temperature by 25° and check for doneness early. Lighter-colored aluminum pans with a dull finish are ideal for baking since they absorb and conduct heat evenly.

YOU FROST CAKES
while they're still warm.

THE RESULT

A crumb-filled layer of frosting

Criminal

Model citizen

THE FIX

Even if you're in a hurry or just eager to dig into a freshly baked cake, it's worth the wait to let it cool. If you frost too soon after it has come out of the oven, crumbs and pieces of the tender, still-warm cake will speckle the frosting. **Let cake layers cool completely before frosting,** or freeze the cake overnight. The layers will retain their freshness and be nice and firm for optimal results. Another way to avoid a crumb-filled frosting: Apply a thin layer of frosting—known as a crumb coat—to seal in those crumbs, and allow it to set in the fridge for 15 minutes before applying the rest.

YOU BEAT CHEESECAKE BATTER
until it's fluffy.

THE RESULT

Your cake has cracks.

Not-so-grand canyon

THE FIX

One cause of the cracks is overbeating the cream cheese mixture, the eggs, or both. **Excess beating causes the mixture to get really fluffy. It then falls as it cools, creating those ravine-like cracks that speckle the cake's surface.** Make sure the cream cheese is at room temperature before you begin so there's less need for heavy mixing.

Another cause is overcooking. It's easy to do since cheesecake often still looks underdone when it's time to turn off the oven. Recipes usually read something like this: "Cook until the cheesecake center barely moves when pan is touched." When it comes to cheesecakes, the center is actually the 3-inch area in the middle of the cake, and it should slightly jiggle when you shake the pan to test doneness.

YOU ROLL OUT THE
pie dough first.

THE RESULT

Mealy crust

THE FIX

To get the quintessential flakiness that defines a perfect piecrust, the dough has to stay cold. Here's how it works: Pie dough recipes usually call for the fat (butter or shortening) to be cut into the dry ingredients using a pastry blender or two knives, which distributes small bits of fat coated in dry ingredients throughout the mixture. While the crust bakes, those bits of fat melt, giving off steam and creating flaky layers. **When the dough gets warm before making it to the oven, the bits start melding together too soon, altering the consistency of the crust and preventing the formation of the flaky layers.** Once the pie dough is rolled out, chill it for 30 minutes before adding the filling.

YOU FORGET TO SEAL
and vent the piecrust.

THE RESULT

Overflow

Venting and sealing are crucial pie-making steps. As the pie bakes, steam is created from the moisture in the filling, causing it and the crust on top to expand. **Properly sealing the edges keeps the filling from leaking out and creating a sticky mess beneath the pie and in the oven, while the vents in the top allow built-up steam to escape.** For added insurance, place the pie plate on a foil-lined baking sheet in case some filling does bubble over.

Busted!

YOU USE OVERRIPE FRUIT
in cobblers and crisps.

Mushy applesauce

THE RESULT

The fruit disintegrates and becomes mushy.

THE FIX

The difference between perfectly ripe and overripe can be a fine line, but when it comes to cobblers and crisps, the distinction is important. **Fruit at the peak of freshness will not only deliver optimum flavor, but it will also hold its shape better, leaving you with sweet, tender pieces after cooking.** Soft, overripe fruit will break down further in the heat of the oven, leaving you with a mushy filling.

WHEN MAKING PUDDING, you add hot milk to the eggs.

THE RESULT

Pudding that looks like porridge

THE FIX

A proper pudding has a rich, velvety texture that makes you yearn for childhood—unless you were ever given a watery pile of pudding with scrambled egg–like pieces suspended in a milky broth. The problem is a failure to temper, the critical heat-control technique that basically acclimates eggs to a higher heat.

The solution: **Slowly whisk a thin stream of the hot milk mixture into beaten raw eggs in a bowl.** Tempering will heat the eggs gradually without cooking them completely. The milk-egg mixture can then be returned to the pan and cooked as the recipe requires. Be patient while cooking, though: If you crank up the heat after tempering, you can still wreck things, even with the inclusion of flour or cornstarch for stabilization. A small jump in the pudding's temperature can lead to coagulation.

YOU FORGET TO COVER
phyllo dough.

THE RESULT

Brittle, cracked, unusable dough

THE FIX

Phyllo must be handled with care. The paper-thin sheets are delicate and can dry out easily, leaving you with dough that isn't good for pastries, tarts, or anything else. Before beginning, thaw the phyllo in the refrigerator overnight. (You can store the unused portion in plastic wrap, and keep it in the fridge for up to a week.) **To prevent it from drying out, work with one or two sheets at a time and keep the rest covered with a damp towel.** If the phyllo tears as you're working with it, spray the tear with cooking spray as a quick fix to bond the torn dough.

I'm parched!

YOU PILE WET TOPPINGS
on pizza crust.

THE RESULT

A soggy bottom

THE FIX

The crust is undeniably one of the best parts of homemade pizza. To get the coveted golden-brown crust, you need to give pizza dough some love. There are two ways. **The first option: Prebake the crust.** This is helpful if you're topping the pizza with particularly wet ingredients like fresh tomatoes that will release water as the pizza cooks. To prebake, roll out the dough onto a baking sheet and place it in a preheated oven for 2 to 3 minutes. This initial time in the oven seals the dough and prevents moisture from penetrating it.

    The second option: Place the pizza dough on a preheated baking sheet or pizza stone. The heat beneath the dough gives it a jump start in the oven, creating a brown rather than soggy crust. To preheat the pan, place it in the oven when you set the temperature. It'll be ready to go when you are. Sprinkling the pan with cornmeal before the dough goes on is also helpful. Cornmeal stops the dough from sticking to the pan, reducing moisture absorption.

WHEN MAKING YEAST BREAD,
you don't check the temp.

THE RESULT

Lifeless loaves

Droopy

Dreamy

THE FIX

Yeast bread has a reputation for being complicated and temperamental, with a wrong step yielding flat dough. The secret is in the yeast, a live, active organism that must be kept happy. **Yeast will only perform correctly in temperatures that allow it to thrive and multiply.** The first step: Dissolve yeast in water that's the correct temperature—100° to 110°. Water that is too cold will prohibit growth, and water that is too hot will kill the yeast. Use a thermometer until you feel comfortable recognizing the target temperature. Then, after the dough has been kneaded, keep it in a warm area (85°), free from drafts, for maximum yeast activity. One way to achieve this is to cover the dough and place it in a cool oven above a bowl or pan filled with boiling water.

If the bread is *still* not rising, the yeast may have expired. To check it, dissolve one package of yeast in warm water. If the mixture produces foam, the yeast is still good. If not, it's time to buy some more.

OOPS!

GRILLING

YOU DON'T PREHEAT
the grill.

THE RESULT

You incinerate the food.

THE FIX

Whether you're grilling with gas or charcoal, a steady, hot fire is crucial. **Once the grill is turned on (or the coals are dumped beneath the grate), always close the lid and allow the grill to get hot.** An eager griller may be tempted to skip this step, but if the heat doesn't have time to stabilize at the correct temperature, food will burn before it cooks through. As a general rule, allow about 10 minutes for a gas grill to heat up and about 30 to 40 minutes for charcoal.

YOU SKIP ADDING
more coals.

THE RESULT

The fire fizzles out.

THE FIX

With larger cuts of meat that require hours over indirect heat, maintaining the coals is crucial. To keep the fire at a steady temperature over a long period of time, you'll need to add new coals while cooking. **It depends on the grill and the type of charcoal, but in general, you'll need to add about 10 to 15 briquettes every 45 minutes to an hour.** Standard briquettes take about 20 minutes to heat up, so plan ahead and add them 20 minutes before you need them. Or try using lump charcoal instead of more common briquettes. Lump charcoal burns hotter and faster, and as a bonus, you'll avoid the fillers and binders used in briquettes. Of course, with gas grills, none of this is an issue.

Adjusting the air vents will give you even more heat control. The more air flowing into the grill, the hotter the fire will burn.

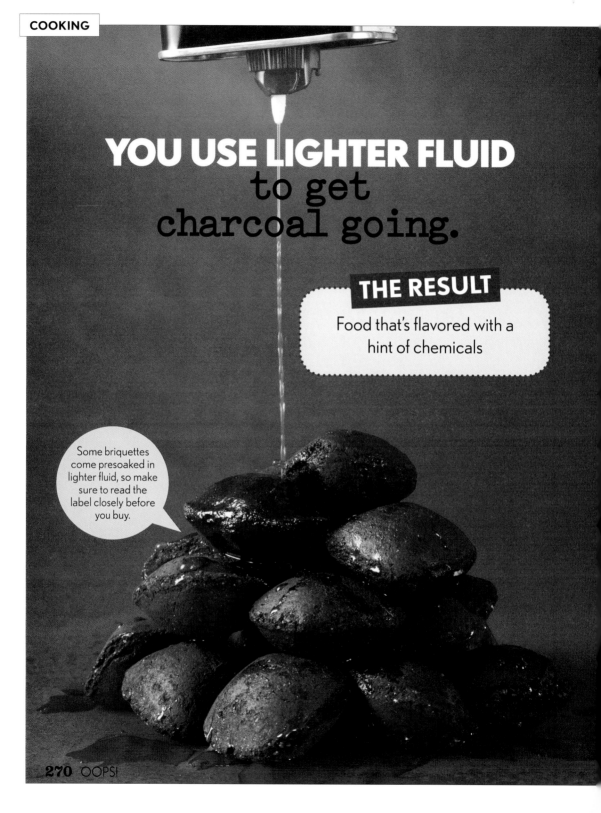

THE FIX

When stomachs are rumbling, a hit of lighter fluid on the coals to give them a jump start can seem like an easy shortcut. Resist. **The time you save with lighter fluid isn't worth the bitter taste it leaves behind, and no sauce, marinade, or rub can hide it.** To start a charcoal fire, all you need is a chimney starter and some newspaper. Stuff the newspaper in the bottom of the chimney starter, place charcoal in the top, and light the paper. The coals will be ready in about 30 minutes.

YOU GRILL
over flames.

THE RESULT

Meat that's both charred and undercooked, with a sooty residue to boot

THE FIX

Maintaining an even, powerful heat is important for great grilling, and cooking over embers is the key to an even heat. As a rule, **charcoal and wood fires should be burned down to glowing embers before food ever touches the grate.** Allow about 30 minutes from the time you light the fire, and wait until the coals have a bright-red glow with a gray, ashy look. It may take some time, but don't rush: Cooking over flames will scorch food quickly and unevenly, leaving you with charred and inedible results.

YOU DON'T CLEAN
the grate every time.

THE RESULT

The food sticks.

Clean release

THE FIX

If you're prying food off the grill every time, chances are there's one crucial thing you *aren't* doing: cleaning that grill. **Before and after each grill session, clean the grates thoroughly with a wire brush.** (A brass-bristle brush is best, since steel bristles can damage the enamel finish of some grates. Make sure the bristles are in good repair—you don't want wayward bristles making their way into the food.) Each time you grill, preheat the rack with all burners on high for 10 to 15 minutes to incinerate any remaining residue from the last cookout, making it easy to clean off. Then, brush the grates vigorously with a grill brush so they're smooth and free from any stuck-on food. Finally, make sure to oil both the grates and the food. Cleaning the grill isn't just to prevent sticking. You'll also get the best flavors when you're not incorporating leftover bits from previous cookouts.

Uh oh

YOU COAT THE GRILL RACKS
with cooking spray while they're over the fire.

THE RESULT

Torched food

THE FIX

Just don't do it. Sudden flare-ups will not only scorch the food, but they'll also put you at risk for getting burned. For safe grilling, **carefully remove the grill racks from the fire, and then coat them with cooking spray or use a paper towel coated in oil to easily grease them** without leaving behind an oily mess. Coating the food with cooking spray or oil will also help keep it from sticking to the grates without causing any safety hazards. Choose an oil with a high smoke point (such as peanut oil).

Whoa!

YOU FORGET ABOUT
the fat in meats.

THE FIX

Most flare-ups are caused by fat dripping onto the fire, which makes them easy to avoid. **Carefully trimming all excess fat from the outside of meats before putting them on the grill or opting for leaner cuts of ground beef when making burgers will prevent most flare-ups.** Flames are inevitable, however, so when cooking fattier cuts or burgers made with ground meat higher in fat, be prepared with an area of indirect heat where you can move food to safety.

Kill a flare-up with a quick spritz of water. Be sparing: Anything more than a mist could cause ashes to float onto the food.

THE RESULT

Flare-ups

Most food cooks best with a combination of direct and indirect heat—but even when you plan on cooking over direct heat only, don't cover 100% of the grill. **It's always a good idea to leave yourself an open space so you can reposition food if flare-ups occur.** You should aim to have no more than two-thirds of the grill covered.

Room to breathe

YOU USE
short tongs.

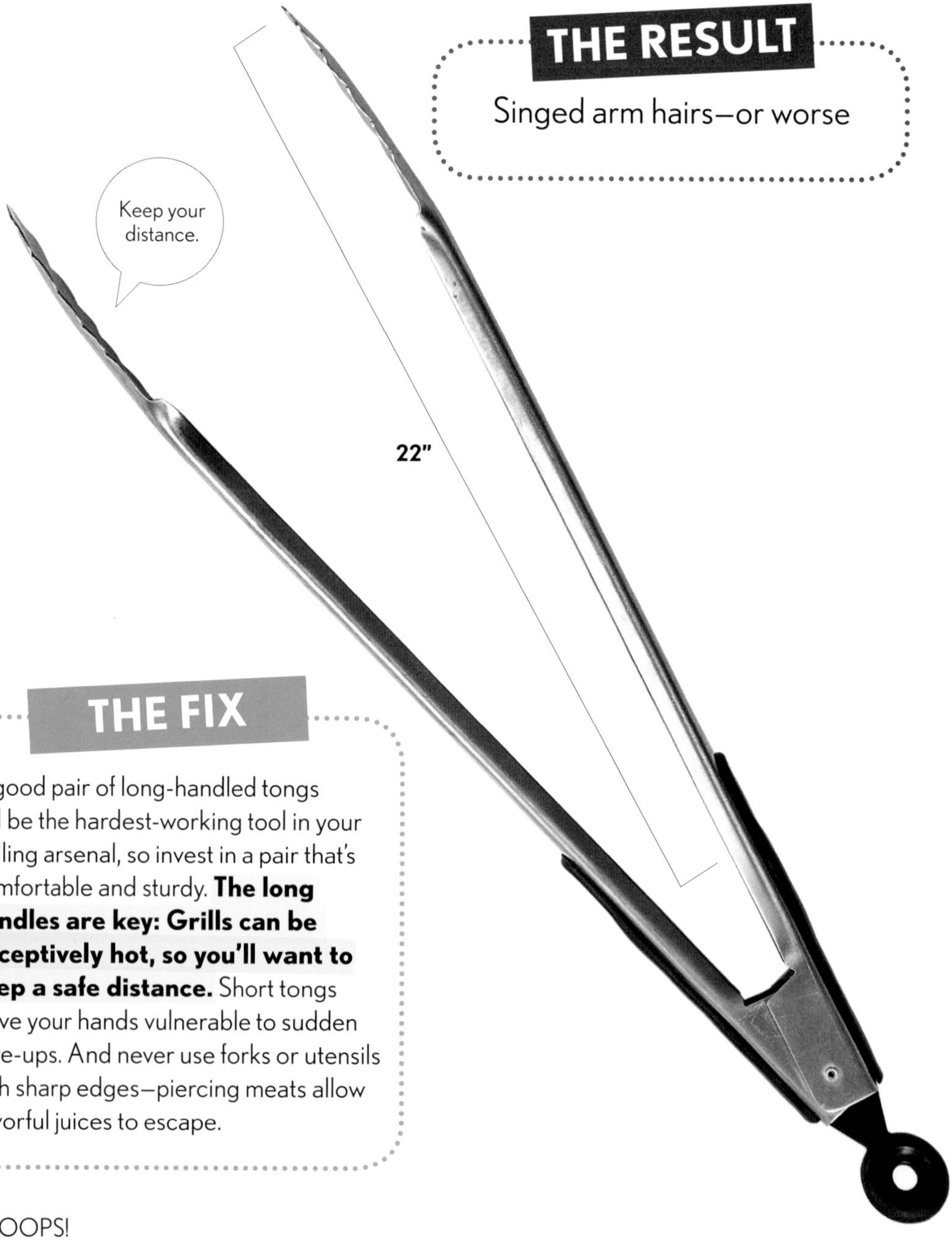

Keep your distance.

THE RESULT

Singed arm hairs—or worse

22"

THE FIX

A good pair of long-handled tongs will be the hardest-working tool in your grilling arsenal, so invest in a pair that's comfortable and sturdy. **The long handles are key: Grills can be deceptively hot, so you'll want to keep a safe distance.** Short tongs leave your hands vulnerable to sudden flare-ups. And never use forks or utensils with sharp edges—piercing meats allow flavorful juices to escape.

YOU GRILL WITH
dry wooden skewers.

THE RESULT

The skewers blacken and burn.

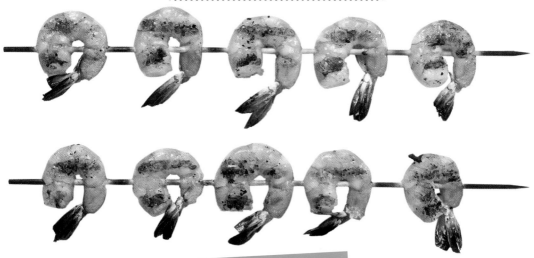

THE FIX

The kebabs may be perfectly cooked masterpieces, but the presentation is less than stellar when the skewers are blackened, sooty sticks. This is an easy fix: **Soak the skewers in water for about 30 minutes before assembling the kebabs** for beautiful results. You can also freeze the skewers in a bag after soaking them so they're ready to go when you are.

YOU THOROUGHLY MIX
burger patties.

Mistreated meat

THE RESULT

Tough, dense burgers

Handled with care

THE FIX

Your own two hands are the ideal tools for shaping burgers, but **too much manhandling will leave you with a finished product that's tough, not tender.** For perfect patties, use a light touch and be careful not to compact the meat as you shape the patties. Work the ingredients evenly and lightly, enough to form a sturdy patty but no longer than necessary. Use your thumb to make a small indentation in the center of each patty before tossing it on the grill. Burgers swell in the middle as they heat up, so this trick will help them hold their shape and cook evenly.

YOU COOK TURKEY BURGERS
like regular hamburgers.

THE RESULT

Burgers that are
parched pucks

Dry as a
desert

THE FIX

A well-made turkey burger is a delicious alternative to the bovine kind—but it needs a little more attention than its red-meat counterpart. The high heat dries out meat quickly, so turkey with its lower fat content, can easily turn to sawdust on the grill. The answer: **Add in some healthy fat with olive oil.** Stirring in two tablespoons of olive oil per pound of ground turkey will keep burgers moist and juicy. Experiment with other moisture-rich stir-ins, such as sautéed onions or pureed eggplant, for juicy burgers with an extra kick of flavor.

Marvelously
moist

YOU DON'T PREP THE GRILL
for fish.

Calamity

THE RESULT

The fish falls apart.

Clean lift

THE FIX

Grilled fish makes for a delicious, healthy meal, but many backyard chefs give the seafood counter a wide berth for fear of disastrous results: fillets that cling to the grill rack and break into little pieces when you try to flip them. A grimy grill, insufficient heat, and the wrong fish are all often to blame.

Stickage prevention starts at the store. **Skip delicate, flaky fish such as tilapia, cod, or flounder (unless you're using a fish basket), and go with firmer-fleshed fish, such as salmon, tuna, or swordfish.** Pat the fillets dry with paper towels before grill time. Now prep the grill: Set the rack over a hot fire for 10 to 15 minutes to burn away lingering debris, and then scrub thoroughly with a grill brush. Carefully lift the rack and coat with cooking spray or swab with oil using wadded paper towels held with tongs (see page 276). Finally, back off—let the fillets cook undisturbed for a few minutes. When it's time to flip, they'll release cleanly. And don't use tongs for fish. A spatula is less likely to tear the fillets.

YOU GRILL LARGE CUTS
of meat quickly.

THE RESULT

A raw center

20 minutes isn't enough.

Choosing the best cut of meat depends on many factors: the recipe, your price range, the occasion. One major factor is your dinner deadline. If you want to get a meal on the table quickly, then a pork shoulder isn't the ideal cut. It's a thick piece of meat that takes hours to cook properly. **If time isn't on your side, opt for smaller cuts** like pork tenderloin, pork chops, chicken breasts and thighs, and fish fillets that will cook quickly over medium-high to high heat.

20 minutes to pork chop perfection

YOU ALWAYS MARINATE MEATS
overnight.

THE RESULT

Fish and seafood are overly salty and tough; meats are mushy and grainy.

Gross grey

Pretty in pink

THE FIX

Marinating is a simple and effective way to impart all kinds of flavors to a cookout. But like many things, it's best in moderation. Acidic marinades made with citrus, wine, and vinegar can compromise the texture and overwhelm the subtle flavors of the meat if left on too long. **In general, small or delicate foods need only 15 to 30 minutes to soak up the flavors, and even the toughest cuts of meat don't need more than 12 hours.** Salt and other delicate seasonings tend to get lost in a strong marinade (see page 146). Get the most out of seasonings by adding them directly to the meat after marinating, not to the marinade. Plan ahead (but not too far ahead) to avoid an overmarinated mess.

YOU FLIP MEAT
frequently.

THE RESULT

Dried-out, tough meat with barely-there grill marks

THE FIX

It's hard to resist poking and prodding meat to try to check on how it's doing. But when the fire is good and hot and the food is cooking, step away: **Once a piece of meat is on the grill, avoid moving it before it's ready so the outside develops a good char.** To test when a burger is ready to flip, slip the edge of a spatula under the edge of the burger and lift up gently. If the meat is sticking to the grate, let it be and try again a minute later. If the grate is properly cleaned and oiled, the food should lift up easily when it's ready to flip.

YOU CHECK THE DONENESS OF MEATS
by cutting into them.

Escape!

THE RESULT

Unattractive presentation (who wants a steak with a big slice down the middle?) and dry meat

House arrest

THE FIX

Put down that knife! Juices settle in the center of a piece of meat as it cooks, and they need time to redistribute after coming off the grill. **When you slice into meat to check doneness, all those yummy juices seep right out.** Allow at least 5 to 10 minutes for meat to rest before cutting into it, and test for doneness with a meat thermometer instead of a knife. Place the thermometer in the thickest part of the meat, and for an accurate reading, make sure you're not touching bone, fat, gristle, or the filling in stuffed meat. Always err on the side of undercooking. You can easily throw it back on the grill for a few minutes, but once it's overcooked, there's no going back.

YOU COOK CHICKEN
over direct heat.

THE RESULT

Chicken breasts that are black on the outside and pink in the middle

THE FIX

Perfectly grilled chicken (think crispy, browned skin and juicy meat) requires grilling over indirect heat. Start by establishing two temperature zones: For a gas grill, set one side to medium-high and the other to low; for charcoal, build a fire on one side of the grill. Start the bone-in, skin-on chicken, skin side up, on the low- or no-heat side, and cover the grill. After a few minutes, flip the meat skin side down. Point the breasts' thicker ends toward the hot side to help them cook evenly. Cover and grill for about 25 minutes. When the meat is done (165° at the thickest part of the breast), crisp the skin on the hot side for a minute or two, moving it as needed to avoid flare-ups.

YOU START BASTING
with barbecue sauce immediately.

THE RESULT

Sugary sauces scorch.

THE FIX

Sugar burns very quickly over high heat. **When grilling with sweet, sugar-based sauces (several kinds of barbecue sauces fall into this category), always add them at the end of the cooking time** (within the last 15 to 20 minutes), or use them when cooking over indirect heat. When using leftover marinade, don't baste during the last 5 minutes of grill time, or you might not allow enough time for the heat to kill any bacteria that may be present..

YOU PUT ALL vegetables directly on the grate.

THE RESULT

Small items fall through the grate.

Living on the edge

Grilling isn't just for hefty hunks of meat. Everything from asparagus to scallops can benefit from time on the grill, so don't let the grate hold you back. Skewers are often helpful, but they aren't your only option. **A grill basket is the easiest way to infuse small bites with smoky flavor.** Choose a nonstick version, and you can simply toss in smaller or more delicate food for hassle-free grilling.

YOU DON'T SOAK
the wood chips.

THE RESULT

Smoked meats that aren't that smoky

Soaked and ready to smoke

Smoking meat requires cooking over a lower temperature (200° to 225°) for a longer period of time, giving the food time to absorb all those delicious, smoky flavors. On a gas grill, it can be impossible to get the heat down to the ideal smoking temperature range. In that case, smoke on the lowest heat level the grill can maintain, and reduce the cooking time. **To get the most smoke, soak wood chips in water for 30 minutes,** and then place the drained chips on the hot coals. Heat the wood chips for 10 minutes or until they start letting off smoke before putting food on the grill. On a gas grill, place the soaked chips in a smoker box or on a piece of heavy-duty foil, loosely fold it up, and then poke about six holes in the top to allow smoke to escape. Turn on the burner at one end of the grill, and arrange the pouch close to that burner. Place an aluminum foil pan filled with water on the unheated side of the grill, replace the grill racks and arrange the food on the rack directly above the aluminum foil pan.

Still not smoky enough? Try experimenting with stronger-flavored woods such as oak or mesquite. Avoid soft woods like pine, spruce, or other evergreens, which will produce a sooty, unpleasant smoke.

nutritional analysis:
what the numbers mean for you

To interpret the nutritional analysis in *Cooking Light Oops!*, use the figures below as a daily reference guide. One size doesn't fit all, so take lifestyle, age, and circumstances into consideration. For example, pregnant or breast-feeding women need more protein, calories, and calcium. Go to choosemyplate.gov for your own individualized plan.

IN OUR NUTRITIONAL ANALYSIS, WE USE THESE ABBREVIATIONS

sat	saturated fat	**CHOL**	cholesterol
mono	monounsaturated fat	**CALC**	calcium
poly	polyunsaturated fat	**g**	gram
CARB	carbohydrates	**mg**	milligram

DAILY NUTRITION GUIDE

	Women ages 25 to 50	Women over 50	Men ages 25 to 50	Men over 50
Calories	2,000	2,000 or less	2,700	2,500
Protein	50g	50g or less	63g	60g
Fat	65g or less	65g or less	88g or less	83g or less
Saturated Fat	20g or less	20g or less	27g or less	25g or less
Carbohydrates	304g	304g	410g	375g
Fiber	25g to 35g	25g to 35g	25g to 35g	25g to 35g
Cholesterol	300mg or less	300mg or less	300mg or less	300mg or less
Iron	18mg	8mg	8mg	8mg
Sodium	2,300mg or less	1,500mg or less	2,300mg or less	1,500mg or less
Calcium	1,000mg	1,200mg	1,000mg	1,000mg

The nutritional values used in our calculations either come from The Food Processor, Version 10.4 (ESHA Research), or are provided by food manufacturers.

metric equivalents

The information in the following charts is provided to help cooks outside the United States successfully use the recipes in this book. All equivalents are approximate.

COOKING/OVEN TEMPERATURES

	Fahrenheit	Celsius	Gas Mark
Freeze Water	32° F	0° C	
Room Temp.	68° F	20° C	
Boil Water	212° F	100° C	
Bake	325° F	160° C	3
	350° F	180° C	4
	375° F	190° C	5
	400° F	200° C	6
	425° F	220° C	7
	450° F	230° C	8
Broil			Grill

LIQUID INGREDIENTS BY VOLUME

¼ tsp	=					1 ml		
½ tsp	=					2 ml		
1 tsp	=					5 ml		
3 tsp	=	1 tbl	=	½ fl oz	=	15 ml		
2 tbls	=	⅛ cup	=	1 fl oz	=	30 ml		
4 tbls	=	¼ cup	=	2 fl oz	=	60 ml		
5⅓ tbls	=	⅓ cup	=	3 fl oz	=	80 ml		
8 tbls	=	½ cup	=	4 fl oz	=	120 ml		
10⅔ tbls	=	⅔ cup	=	5 fl oz	=	160 ml		
12 tbls	=	¾ cup	=	6 fl oz	=	180 ml		
16 tbls	=	1 cup	=	8 fl oz	=	240 ml		
1 pt	=	2 cups	=	16 fl oz	=	480 ml		
1 qt	=	4 cups	=	32 fl oz	=	960 ml		
				33 fl oz	=	1000 ml	=	1 l

DRY INGREDIENTS BY WEIGHT

To convert ounces to grams, multiply the number of ounces by 30.

1 oz	=	¹⁄₁₆ lb	=	30g
4 oz	=	¼ lb	=	120g
8 oz	=	½ lb	=	240g
12 oz	=	¾ lb	=	360g
16 oz	=	1 lb	=	480g

LENGTH

To convert inches to centimeters, multiply the number of inches by 2.5.

1 in	=					2.5 cm		
6 in	=	½ ft			=	15 cm		
12 in	=	1 ft			=	30 cm		
36 in	=	3 ft	=	1 yd	=	90 cm		
40 in	=					100 cm	=	1 m

EQUIVALENTS FOR DIFFERENT TYPES OF INGREDIENTS

Standard Cup	Fine Powder (ex. flour)	Grain (ex. rice)	Granular (ex. sugar)	Liquid Solids (ex. butter)	Liquid (ex. milk)
1	140g	150g	190g	200g	240ml
¾	105g	113g	143g	150g	180ml
⅔	93g	100g	125g	133g	160ml
½	70g	75g	95g	100g	120ml
⅓	47g	50g	63g	67g	80ml
¼	35g	38g	48g	50g	60ml
⅛	18g	19g	24g	25g	30ml

INDEX